Desiring
God

Meditations for the gay man and other edgy people

Rev. Dr. Arno Steen Andreasen

ARCHWAY
PUBLISHING

Archway Publishing books may be ordered through booksellers or by contacting:

Archway Publishing
1663 Liberty Drive
Bloomington, IN 47403
www.archwaypublishing.com
844-669-3957

ISBN: 978-1-4808-9680-2 (sc)
ISBN: 978-1-4808-9681-9 (e)

Library of Congress Control Number: 2020918574

Print information available on the last page.

Archway Publishing rev. date: 10/29/2020

"We come to God through our imperfections
and wounds not by moral achievements."

Richard Rohr

Contents

Why?

THIS IS MY book of lamentations. It is a book of pain and frustrations as well as joy, hope, and God's grace.

Inspired by the Psalms, I went back to the Bible to find myself and to find healing, and salvation. I have mirrored my life journey in different Bible texts. Looking for something to cling onto, I found the God of love.

As you read through this book, you will read about a whole range of human emotions just like in the Psalms. I may be furious, but at the end of the reflection, I may have found new faith and trust in the God who turns evil into good. A God who is not far away, but who is at our right hand (Psalm 16:8). It is also a God who is not sorting everything out with a snap of His fingers. For me some of His solutions were quite different to what I would have preferred and prayed for. But He is there, and He was there.

I am reminded of Joseph's conclusion after many years of hardship in Egypt, *"Even though you planned evil against me, God planned good to come out of it. This was to keep many people alive, as he is doing now"* (Genesis 50:20, God's Word Translation).

Sometimes our lives are messy. Mine was put on pause as practically everything changed over a short period of time. This is my story. I wrote these reflections before everything has been sorted out, as

I wanted a testimony of my experience of God walking with me through the wilderness. There are books telling the stories of many wonderful breakthroughs. Writing about faith in hindsight is easy, but I needed faith to get through the darkest valley (Psalm 23:4). I hope this book will help you in whatever situation you may find yourself.

May you have a wonderful revelation of the gracious God of love. His name is Jesus.

Blessings

Arno

Desire – Yes Please

Song of Songs 7 (The Passion Translation)

(The Bridegroom-King):

1 How beautiful on the mountains are the sandaled feet of this one bringing such good news. You are truly royalty! The way you walk so gracefully in my ways displays such dignity. You are truly the poetry of God – his very handiwork.

2-3 Out of your innermost being is flowing the fullness of my Spirit – never failing to satisfy. Within your womb there is a birthing of harvest wheat; they are the sons and daughters nurtured by the purity you impart. How gracious you have become!

4 Your life stands tall like a tower, like a shining light on a hill. Your revelation eyes are pure, like pools of refreshing – sparkling light for a multitude. Such discernment surrounds you, protecting you from the enemy's advance.

5 Redeeming love crowns you as royalty. Your thoughts are full of life, wisdom, and virtue. Even a king is held captive by your beauty.

6 How delicious is your fair beauty; it cannot be described as I count the delights you bring to me. Love has become the greatest.

7 You stand in victory above the rest, stately and secure as you share with me your vineyard of love.

8 Now I decree, I will ascend and arise I will take hold of you with power, possessing every part of my fruitful bride. Your love I will drink as wine, and your words will be mine.

9 For your kisses of love are exhilarating, more than any delight I've known before. Your kisses of love awaken even the lips of sleeping ones.

(The Shulamite Bride):

10 Now I know that I am filled with my beloved and all his desires are fulfilled in me.

11 Come away, my lover. Come with me to the far away fields. We will run away together to the forgotten places and show them redeeming love.

12 Let us arise and run to the vineyard of your people and see if the budding vines of love are not in bloom. We will discover if their passion is awakened. There I will display my love for you.

13 The love apples are in bloom, sending forth their fragrance of spring. The rarest of fruits are found at our doors - the new as well as the old. I have stored them for you, my lover-friend.

JESUS, YOU ARE SO crazy. You say so many sweet nothings to me. Your love is overwhelming. When you see me, you break out in song (7:1). You see it as good news, when I turn to you and want to follow you in all my weakness and frailty. You burst out in song like the angels when a sinner repents. My repentance, my turning around to face you, makes you happy. Imagine that!

The God of the universe cares if I follow my own way or if we walk together. You are waiting for me in the same way as the father was waiting and hoping for the return of the prodigal son. Maybe I am a prodigal, a person wasting my life on irrelevant pursuits, but I see that you do not care as long as you see me coming. It does not matter if I come slowly or walk quickly as long as I am on the Way.

I am reminded of my dog when I was a child. She was always happy to see me, no matter if I had been away for days or for a minute. She just loved me unconditionally and expressed her happiness without restraint. I long for more unconditional love.

God you are so much more than my little dog and still you have no problem showing your love and affection for me. You do not hide your affection. You do not hide your words of love. You do not care what others think. Your concern is for me to hear your voice, and to know that I am loved through and through.

You call me royal and you make me feel like royalty the way you treat me (7:1). You see nobody but me and yet you love all of creation, because you are love (1 John 4:8). You have the unique ability to make me feel special, even though I have been trained to understand that I should fear you, fear judgement, and fear damnation. All the pain of the classic interpretations of the Bible melts away in your love and I feel safe, safe in the love that casts out all fear, not least the fear of God, of sin and of death.

I do not know how to behave in your presence, and yet you think I walk with dignity. I feel that I am just a clumsy guy trying my best, but you see something else. You see a child of God, but I have learnt to see my failings and my shame. I have learnt to focus on all the bad stuff, so it is different and weird to know that you think that I behave with dignity like a true royal. Do you have any idea how mind-boggling it is to be invited to your courts? It is a dream come true, yet scary. Maybe you will think that I am a fraud, not good enough, and not holy enough. Thoughts go through my mind, and yet your words caress me. They soothe my soul and quiet my fears.

And the Bible calls me *"poetry of God!"* (7:1). Your life is touching my heart, your words stir my soul and your beauty heals my wounded body. You see handiwork, where I see a worn-out body and a damaged soul. You see somebody fearfully and wonderfully made, while I see my shortcomings and all my diagnoses including the fear of possible ailments not diagnosed yet (Psalm 139:13-14). How freeing and healing that is. God has not given up on me. I do not have to be young and beautiful for God to love me. I do not need to have a young well-trained body, perfect hair, and look like a success. I do not need to be popular on Grindr or have many likes on Facebook. My God sees work of art: God's work. Lord, give me your eyes to see, so I may honour the Temple of the Holy Spirit that you have entrusted to me.

Free me from the thoughts of being inadequate, a person who cannot find love because I am not young and perfect, and looking like a Greek god. I am loved for who I am. I need to realise that and dare to take the first step over the mountain of the unknown towards my God and Saviour.

It is amazing to hear that I am truly a Temple of your Holy Spirit and that God Himself is nourished by the Holy Spirit flowing from my life (7:2). Lord, I am longing for more of your Spirit working in my life and I have often focused on praying for power to be released. Power to heal, save, and deliver, but you are asking me to let the Holy Spirit flow through me to satisfy you! You are asking me to let the Spirit of Jesus fill me, and touch my inner man, my soul, my identity. You are asking me to be transformed by letting the Spirit grow and flow in my life. I need to learn to let go. Instead I try to protect my innermost being. It is a vulnerable place for me. It is a place that has been bruised and broken. For most of my life there has been a fight over that deep inner space.

I thought my inner man was evil and no good even though I do not really believe in the total depravity of mankind. For some reason, I still believed that I was so rotten to the core that I had nothing, really nothing to offer to God or the world. I tried through education, hard work and successful ministry projects to reclaim that core of my life. Maybe having done something good in my life would redeem me, but it did not work. It only wore me out physically and mentally. I became emotionally bankrupt.

What to do then? I knew I could not change myself, and I felt that God did not hear my prayers. I was convinced that I was a disappointment to Him, but what then?

Embracing the Spirit of Jesus and the love of Jesus put me on a new path. This revelation is leading me to the Way, the Truth, and the Life. It is a good Way, because it takes me to Jesus instead of hiding from Him and fearing Jesus or begging Him to be merciful to me an awful sinner.

This Way showed me that I am created in God's image even though I am a gay man. I was not born with a handicap, a mental disorder, or a moral flaw. I was made very good by the hands of the Master (Genesis 1:31). I had come to believe that the opposite of healthy heterosexuality was homosexuality. We were the depraved ones that never stood a real chance in the Divine lottery. Whenever something went wrong in ministry, in our churches, I felt it was my fault. As the Overseer of a network of churches and ministries, my life affected all our work, and being gay was a death sentence for the movement. People would suffer because of me, but how wrong I was. How neurotic I had become because I believed certain Christian preachers, books, and conference speakers.

The reality is that I have a God who is satisfied by the work of the Holy Spirit that flows from my life. I have a God who celebrates that something fruitful is flowing from my life and ministry. I am the womb that grows spiritual children (7:2-3). My life and ministry are not in vain, because God blesses His children with the power of the Holy Spirit. The Spirit in me creates. It is the living word taking hold of my life and giving me the chance to make a real difference in people's lives and God is delighted. God says that I "impart purity". Me? Purity? Doesn't God know my heart, my mind, and my desires? The church would not call them pure and yet God is not offended my them. God lets my whole being be used for His glory, and He sees purity despite all my shortcomings.

God, your love is making you blind and I am so happy about that, because I am learning that God's love covers a multitude of sins (1 Peter 4:8). It is starting to register. I have known that verse for such a long time, but I have also developed selective hearing. I know from the popular teaching of the church that grace is only really for straight people, for the majority, the "normal" ones. And yet, I am starting to realise that God is also in love with me, because His love is greater than my shortcomings. His love is not dependent on me behaving in a certain way; being straight-acting as expected by many churches. He loves because God is love. My role is to walk towards that love and let love chip away the pain of my heart, so I can become liberated in Him. Then the Spirit can touch my innermost being because I dare to surrender my life to Him. I dare to follow Him without hesitation. I am welcome on His Way to God.

Letting His Spirit work in me leads to all kinds of results as He tells me that I have become gracious (7:2-3). I want more of that reality in my life, Lord. I want to become a gracious person, gracious to others, forgiving and loving. You have shown me so much grace, given me a new lease of life that enables me to offer some of the same grace to others. Can I do it to my enemies, who threw me into hell with their words? Can I do it to the churches who do not allow me to minister any longer?

I know I cannot do it in my own strength. I am too hurt and angry as I still experience barriers to ministry. So, I have a challenge: How do

I pray, forgive and love the people who tell me that they have a high view of the Bible and therefore I must leave the church? I cannot do it, but the Spirit of God can. So, I try to embrace the God of love, I try to appreciate all that God has done for me. I try to believe that God will turn things around for good. That is His role, not mine. My future ministry does not depend on me or on the people who work against LGBT+ people ministering in the church, it depends on God. Maybe that can help me to be more generous to others, not to mention those who have hurt me and my family. I am learning forgiveness on the run.

It looks to me as if God is gender-blind (7:2-4). We pay so much attention to gender and gender roles, but God is more fluid in His expressions. He has just called me a womb (a female attribute) and now He calls me a tower (a more masculine expression). He also clothes Himself in different attributes. He is both father and a hen. God is Jesus, a male representation, and the Holy Spirit, a feminine word. He is God Almighty which also means God the many breasted one. And, we are created in His image as male and female – as well as eunuchs, and intersex. We produce both male and female sex hormones. God has an integrated personality and so are we because we are created in His likeness. How freeing is that? I do not need to play a macho game, but I can present myself as me and not as a stereotype. I can love red, dance and be excited about the performing arts and that does not make me less of a man, created in God's image.

God is so in love with me that He sees my life standing out from the crowd. It is like a strong tower (7:4)! The vulnerabilities, the weaknesses are always in front of me and yet God sees something different. He notices what is right with our lives, and the difference we have made. He sees it as a strength that I / we did not give up and go under due to the discrimination we have faced. We chose to move on and out. We chose to come out despite the consequences, and it takes guts and courage. Over the years, coming out has become easier in many communities around the world, but it is rarely easy. Coming out is not a one-off event, and some weeks I come out daily.

Personally, I consider if I can just say "Yes" to an invitation to speak at an evangelical church or organisation, or if I need to inquire if they are comfortable in having an out gay man as their guest speaker. Will I be accused of hiding something, if I do not come out to them when approached? Many Christians do care if I am gay as well as a "practising homosexual" or not, and then they tell me that I am the one making my gayness all about sex! I wish Christians would be more focused on what injustices happen in the board room than what I do or don't do in my bedroom.

The Lover of my soul thinks that my life is worth shouting about. As a fellow believer and follower of Jesus, I am salt and light. There are no special categories in the Kingdom of God. If you follow Jesus, then you are light. Your life is worth shouting about, and He wants to shout it out from the roof tops, or over the hills (7:4). When some shout about the dangers of the "gay lifestyle", God is shouting about people becoming strong towers because of His Holy Spirit in their lives. It is God's work, not mine. It is God's accomplishment, not mine. My life is wrapped up in God, and the more I let go of all the different negative voices in my head, the more God can touch my heart and transform my mind.

Walking on the Way, I get more revelations about the words of Jesus and the abundant life we have in Him. This journey allows me to receive new inspiration and have new experiences with the Living God (7:4). I have found that I am more open to His life transforming epiphanies when I am in a love relationship with Jesus, instead of a fear-based relationship.

These mysteries of God become lifegiving to others as we do not do life alone (7:4). Liberating God-words impart life and not just life, but eternal life. Therefore, my life in God is extremely important. Other people are affected by my life even in times where I am stripped of all things. People are always watching and reading our lives. As I am dwelling in God, then I can receive pure revelations that are refreshing and a light for the communities of people around us. How cool is that. God is not stingy with His revelation and His love. As He transforms my mind, He is blessing others too. And this revelation will also protect me from my enemies. I am better able, like a strong tower, to stand when people try to cut me down. I have heard from God and His voice is more important than any other voice. I become increasingly aware how crucial it is for me to hold on to His word and revelations of His love for me. I can stand because of God; I can become stronger because of God.

My freedom comes from God. It is His redeeming love that has put me on a new path (7:5). As He grabbed hold of me, I was taken to His royal palace like a knight rescuing a damsel in distress. We are all in need of our Saviour, nobody more than anybody else. We are all in need of our Saviour King who lifts us out of tough situations, unhealthy environments, and stupid decisions. I need to be lifted out of immaturity and put on the right track. God opens the door to a new reality, as His will is impacting the earth with heavenly realities through our prayers and actions (Matthew 6:10).

I am aware that trusting in God is the beginning of wisdom (Proverbs 9:10), but to hear that my thoughts are "full of life, wisdom and virtue" is something else (7:5). God is yet again transforming me without my knowing. He is doing His work deep within me, so great things leak from my life. How can the Almighty God talk about my thoughts as lifegiving and wise? His thoughts are higher than mine and yet He values what I think (Isaiah 55:8). Such love sets me free. I have something to offer God.

I may wonder if anything good can come from Denmark, but God values the thoughts and reflections of a Danish gay man. And isn't that exactly the foundation of a true loving relationship, that we love the other person with our heart, soul, mind and strength. We value every aspect of their lives. We do not "love the sinner, but hate the sin", but we love the whole person warts and all. We do not compartmentalise our love, we love unconditionally. That is agape love, self-giving love. We may not agree with everything that other people say or do, but we are encouraged to love them anyway. We love God because He loved us first while we were still sinners (1 John 4:19). We do not need to be perfect to deserve love. Love is a gift, love is grace, I just need to receive it and trust the Giver of love as Love never fails (1 Corinthians 13:8).

I am blessed with two daughters. In my mind, they are the best and most incredible girls alive. It does not matter if they see themselves as daddy's girls or not, they are daddy's girls in my eyes. They are the apple of my eye. Even if I disagree with them or get angry, they are still the most precious people in the world. And God thinks the same about us. He is captivated by our beauty (7:5-6).

When I look at myself in the mirror in the morning as I shave, I am not captivated by beauty! Isn't it interesting how perspective is everything? I see beauty in my girls no matter what. As teenagers, they saw pimples and brazes, but I saw my wonderful girls. Because of the love of God, He does not see my shortcomings, the wrinkles, and the salt and pepper hair. Well, the grey hair and the baldness, if I shall be honest. God sees a precious child of God and we only take hold of this through revelation. We can quote Scripture until we are red in the face, but it makes no difference at all. On the other hand, when we receive revelation by His Spirit, we realise that God is someone special and His love for me and for us is special too. He is captivated by my beauty! The body-shaming must sneak away because God sees a body beautiful. He does not see a body out of control, a body scarred by life. He sees His creation, His children. We can value our bodies because God does. We can wave goodbye to all negative words and a harmful body-image because our bodies are a Temple of the Holy Spirit. Our bodies are good in the sight of God and not only good, they are beautiful.

When there is a free flow of love, we feel invincible (7:7). When we are in love, we feel safe, we feel unique. That is why loving, covenanted relationships help us to live longer and stay healthier physically and emotionally. Love transforms lives, and fellowship sustains life. We can more easily cope with the injustices and unfairness of the world as a minority group, when we can share our burdens with the love of our life. We are more victorious together than alone, but there are churches who call our faithful gay relationships for sin, the destruction of the institution of family, and a symbol of the moral decay of our society.

I am so happy that in the *"vineyard of love"* we can stand firm. Together with God and each other, we gain the strength to withstand and to heal from the wounds of damaging words. With God, we can have victory *"above the rest"*. We find peace during battle. It is no longer my role to convince others of my value. The battle is the Lord's (2 Chronicles 20:15).

Sometimes I need to remind myself that without our work in the vineyard of love, I get lost and I get hurt. When that happens, I lose my focus, my worth and the hope for the future. I need to return to God, to His eye-opening words of love.

God is so jealous (Exodus 34:14). Isn't that fun to think about? I thought that jealousy and desires were all bad, but God is an emotional God who cares for us. He not only cares, He loves, and He desires us as a love-struck teenager (7:8)! His hormones are activated when He sees me. He wants to possess us, which sounds a bit creepy, but God is not a control freak, He is the Lover of our souls. He knows that without His love and an intimate relationship with Him, we become like sheep without a shepherd. Our lives disintegrate when separated from our Creator. He so wants to protect me from evil that He wants to do everything in His power to save me from pain. I need such a man in my life. A man to protect me from the world, evil spirits, and sometimes myself. Jesus is that man, but a husband and a healthy marital relationship will also make me stronger, healthier, and safer. Together we have a holy space where we become more than conquerors because of our love for each other.

I can share words of love between my Lover, my God and myself (7:8). Our words become muddled together. I no longer recognise His words from mine. We are one in the Spirit. It reminds me of the novel and film, "Call me by your name." During their love making, they begin to call each other by their own name. The two became one, one unit of love. As they are bound together as one, it does not matter who said what and why. Love is the glue that held them together. They were an emotional unit.

God desires me (7:9). He gets excited by my love for Him. It means something to the Creator God. It feels strange, but He is delighted for all the love we can give back to Him. What a powerful feeling that I matter to God and that God is affected by what I do to and for Him. My service to humanity is like a sweet kiss. When I waste time in His presence through prayer or meditation, it invigorates Him. God comes alive when we dare to love. I think I am getting a glimpse of what it means to worship a Holy God. The God who is not like any other god, because the God of the Bible is love.

"*Now I know*" that I am in God and God is in me (7:10). I am filled with His Spirit, the Spirit of self-giving love. I have a role to play as a Christian gay man, because "*his desires are fulfilled in me.*" I must acknowledge that I have a role to play, so I cannot give up on my faith no matter what is done to me in the name of Christ through His church. I cannot turn away from my love for God just because there are Christians who speak against the LGBT+ communities and talk about us as stereotypes and clichés.

I will no longer take part in "Bible bashing games" or compete with others about *the* correct interpretation of Scripture. I do not need to win any argument or convince others that I am a man of God, that I love God, and that I am not deceived. I do not have to try to convince others that I am an evangelical/red letter, charismatic Christian. What I will do, though, is letting God mould me and help me become more like my Lover. I want that to be the focus of my life now.

Radical Inclusion

Luke 14:12-24 (David Bentley Hart Translation)

12 And to the one who had invited him he said, "When you prepare a luncheon or dinner, do not call to your friends or your brothers or your relatives or your rich neighbours, lest they invite you in return and it becomes a recompense for you.

13 Rather, when you prepare a celebration invite the destitute, the crippled, the lame, the blind,

14 And you shall be blissful, for they have nothing to repay you with; for it will be repaid you in the resurrection of the just."

15, And hearing this, one of those reclining at the table with him, said to him, "Blissful is he who eats bread in the Kingdom of God."

16 And he said to him, "A certain man prepared a great banquet and invited many,

17 And sent out his slave at the hour of the banquet to say to those who had been invited, "Come, because it is ready now."

18 And as one they all began to decline. The first said to him, "I have bought a field, and am forced to go out to see it; I ask you, have me excused."

19 And another said, "I bought a yoke of five oxen, and I am going to make a test of them; I ask you, have me excused."

20 And another said, "I have married a wife and therefore cannot come."

21 And, approaching the slave reported these things to his lord. Then, enraged, the master of the house told his slave, "Go out quickly into the streets and alleys of the city, and bring in here the destitute and crippled and blind and lame."

22 And the slave said, "Lord, what you commanded has been done, and there is still room."

23 And the Lord said to the slave, "Go out to the roads and palings and force them to come in, so that my house may be filled;

24 For I tell you, not one of those men who have been invited shall taste of my banquet."

I HAVE BEEN READING a series of articles in a Danish newspaper about inequality in the nation. Denmark is known for the Scandinavian model; focusing on giving everybody a chance, having one of the best democracies in the world, and having a minimum wage at a level that is significantly higher than most other Western nations. We are used to things being quite good in our nation.

These articles claimed that things are shifting. We have become less welcoming to asylum seekers, and general elections are won or lost based on the party's stand on the issue. We have started to build neighbourhoods for the rich instead of the integrated estates that we are used to, where the rich and the middle classes live side by side, and children are attending the same state schools. Now, we move into areas where there are more people like us because that is where we feel safe. We like the idea of diversity; but embracing it in everyday life seems difficult.

As I was reading these articles, I felt such a need for the church to become the United Nations of a community. The place where people of all backgrounds would feel at home and get to know each other. If society is disintegrating, then the church must become the glue that makes communities work. We can no longer just be the middleclass church, the ethnic church, the LGBT+ church or the evangelical-straight-white church. We have a calling to be radically inclusive and especially when society is pulling us apart.

The Passion Translation says it in this way, "*Stop imitating the ideals and opinions of the culture around you*" (Romans 12:2), and the New International Version offers this translation, "*Do not conform to the pattern of this world.*"

We are called to do church and live in a radically different way. We must not copy others but need to get our act together as we cannot accept and embrace policies and behaviours that are anti-God. That is one of the reasons I love being involved in church. We have the chance to develop alternative communities, so people can see who God is and get a chance to "*taste and see that the Lord is good*" (Psalm 34:8, New International Version).

Jesus was invited to the house of one of the leading Pharisees. They were watching Jesus like hawks (14:1). When reading the fuller story, then it does not sound like the most relaxed time. But Jesus had the ability to use these occasions as teaching opportunities, showing that God is different. Tension would hang in the air as people were challenged to make up their minds. He was not going to play games. There was an authenticity to His behaviour. He did not say one thing to one group of people to please them and something else to another group. There was no spin, only integrity.

This group of Pharisees saw themselves as the VIPs (Very Important Persons) of the religious world. They controlled the synagogues throughout the country, while the Sadducees controlled the Temple, but Jesus refused to conform to the patterns of the religious culture. He was aware that He was invited so they could check him out. He was the new hot thing on the preaching circuit, so it was a real scoop to have Him around, but Jesus did not play by their rule book.

A man with a dropsy entered the house and stood close to Jesus (14:2). In our culture we do not think twice about that, but Jesus knew that the host and his friends would be extremely interested to see, what Jesus would do next. He was the Healer from God after all, but it was a Sabbath day; the day of rest (14:3). It was the perfect setup. If Jesus would heal the man, then He would go against their rules for the Sabbath and therefore He could not be of God. On the other hand, if He did not, then He would not be faithful to His ministry of healing and restoration.

It amazes me how quickly we who read and study the Bible become like the Pharisees in different aspects of Christian theology and living. In the same way as the Pharisees were eager to live holy lives and therefore created rules for people to abide by, so the modern church has developed a tradition for the only true interpretation of God's word. If you dare to wrestle with the Scriptures and come to other conclusions, then you are no good. Then you do not have a high view of the Bible, and you are not a believer of the orthodox faith. You no longer belong to the true believers: the evangelicals, fundamentalists, charismatics, Pentecostals.... you have become liberal and you do not take the teaching of the Bible seriously. I have heard that too many times to count.

Jesus responded to the religious leaders by telling them who they should really invite to their dinner parties. It was not people like Him, but those who were easily forgotten and overlooked. The ones who do not normally get on the guest list as they have nothing to contribute (14:12). This group of people do not add any prestige, or good business deals to the gathering. They do not look religious enough and they may not speak the right "Christianese" either. These hidden saints have all too often been pushed out of fellowship, because they did not add value to other people's social or religious standing.

I remember when we started planting churches in India, I was told that we needed to consider what looked good in the eyes of the pastors from other denominations. I wondered why we should let our church be taken hostage by pastors of other denominations. I thought we could only become good news to this community, if we dared to live radically, and be inspired by the ways of Jesus.

Jesus told them that real Kingdom hosts invite the destitute, the crippled, the lame and the blind - so Jesus could heal them even on a Sabbath (14:13). Deliverance from the oppression of illness or society is always on the top of the Jesus agenda. When we come together, then people are liberated. There is no liberation if we only create churches for the majority groups. Liberation comes, when the powerful give up their power in order to embrace others. Therefore, men step aside when they notice the anointing on women in their churches. Therefore, we make room for the Dalit pastor to lead a congregation that also consists of high cast people like we did in India and Nepal.

In each community this group of people (destitute, crippled, lame, and blind) have different names. The Message Version uses this expression: "The misfits from the wrong side of the tracks." The Passion Translation talks about the "outcasts". Who are the outcasts in your community and in your friendship circle who could use an experience of the radical inclusion of God? His Kingdom is a Kingdom for all His children, who want to join the party.

I remember when my children were very young. It was the birthday of one of my daughters and we had invited the whole class to the party. We wanted to show that everybody was welcome in our home. When the parents came with their children, they said that we were bold (or crazy) to invite so many children to a party. A mother came to thank us for inviting her son. He was not one of the popular children in the class (he was no trouble), so he was never invited to the birthday

parties. He was sad when he did not get invited like the other children. We did not know about this and in our minds, we had done
nothing special. For this family, it was a big thing, that their son was
not uninvited as usual. He had been invited like anybody else and he
felt special. God's invitation is to all, also the ones who are not the
most popular in the class.

One person at the Jesus party got the point: It is always significant
to be invited to join the Jesus movement (14:15) and Jesus used the
situation to make a point (14:16).

People used all kinds of excuses for not being able to join when the
party was ready to begin (14:18-20). The guests may have come to
understand that the riffraff was invited as well, and then there was
no point in spending time with the Jesus movement (the church?).
When you invite widows, orphans, the HIV positive, Tutsis or Hutus,
migrants, the homeless, refugees, LGBT+, then the party is not that
attractive anymore for the power brokers of the world. Diversity does
nothing to our social standing in society, business, or in the faith
community. Christians are sometimes afraid that it might look like
we are compromising our faith if we celebrate God's goodness with
such people.

We can be so afraid of other people's opinions about us that we forget
what the Kingdom is all about. We push away different worshippers
because they are different. We proclaim we welcome all, but have we
listened to our own preaching lately, and do we notice the culture we
have developed? When people show up in our churches, they know
if they are truly welcome or not. As a gay man, I know that churches
tell me that I am welcome (they call themselves inclusive), but I cannot become a leader, I cannot serve in an official capacity, but I am
welcome to come and worship. How can I be free in worship if I am
treated like a second-rate citizen? I can only truly immerse myself in

worship and fellowship in a place where I am accepted, respected, and fully embraced.

Jesus challenged his slave to keep on going (14:21-22). There was room at the table and God is not fuzzy. He looked for followers of all shapes and sizes, not only people who conform to a certain standard chosen by man.

Notice that Jesus walks the talk. He told the Pharisee whom to invite and did exactly that (14:13, 21). Jesus stuck to His values. He did not compromise to look good. He pushed His inclusive agenda when it would have been easier not to. He kept on painting a picture of a God who likes and loves His children. He is eager to gather us from all backgrounds, so we can glue our communities together.

So as usual, Jesus went one step further, saying, *"For I tell you, not one of those men who have been invited shall taste of my banquet"* (14:24). Jesus was probably referring to some of the Jews who did not believe that Gentiles could be saved. Let us take up the challenge, when we are tempted to become the judge of another person's faith as it opens the door for abuse and discrimination: It happens when we embrace the attitude that my faith is of more value than your faith, that I know the true interpretation of Scripture and as a consequence others must abide my ideas, or they are out.

Kingdom people are those who will do anything to get as diverse a group of people as possible together around God's table. This includes the ones, we disagree with. God is not afraid of His reputation, so let us try to catch His Spirit and help others to become part of our church fellowships, so they can experience the transforming power of God's love as well. We are all equals around the table, there is no hierarchy, and everybody is welcome to minister in the power of the Holy Spirit. We do believe in the priesthood of all believers after all!

Being on Fire for God (Stephen)

Acts 7:54 – 8:3, 9:1-5 (David Bentley Hart Translation)

54 And, hearing these things, they were cut to their hearts, and ground their teeth at him.

55 But, being full of a Holy Spirit, gazing into the sky, he saw God's glory, and Jesus standing at God's right hand,

56 And he said, "Look, I see the heavens opened and the Son of Man standing at God's right hand."

57 And crying out with a loud voice they covered their ears and rushed upon him, all in one mind,

58 And throwing him outside the city they stoned him, and the witnesses shed their robes at the feet of a young man called Saul,

59 And they stoned Stephen, who prayed and said, "Lord Jesus, receive my spirit."

60 And going down on his knees he cried with a loud voice, "Lord, do not charge them with this sin." And saying this he fell asleep.

8:1 And there was Saul, approving of his destruction. And on that day a great persecution broke out against the assembly in Jerusalem. And all but the Apostles were dispersed throughout the territories of Judea and Samaria.

2 And devout men helped to bear Stephen away and performed loud lamentations over him.

3 But Saul wreaked havoc upon the assembly, entering house after house, hauling off both men and women and delivered them to prison.

9:1 But Saul, still snorting out menaces and slaughter at the Lord's disciples, approaching the chief priest,

2 Requested letters from him to Damascus for the synagogues, so that if he discovered any persons belonging to the Way he might lead them in bonds to Jerusalem, men and women alike.

3 Now, as he journeyed, it happened that he drew near Damascus, and suddenly their flashed around him a light from the sky,

4 And falling upon the ground he heard a voice saying to him, "Saul, Saul, why do you persecute me?"

5 And he said, "Lord, who are you?" And he said, "I am Jesus, whom you persecute…

WHEN I BECAME a Christian, it was important to be on fire for God. It was part and parcel of showing that you had a genuine faith and that you wanted to do business with God. We would pray for the fire to come down, for the Spirit of God to equip us and send us out. We stood in the streets of London proclaiming the goodness of God or laid down on the pavement to repent for the sins of the city, and so on. Our longing for God was great, and we put our heart and soul into it. We would shout in those prayer meetings, stamp our feet, and tell the north, south, east, and west to let go of the people of the city, so they could see God.

It was a great time in many ways. Feeling that I was on the spiritual cutting edge was thrilling. There were so many interesting speakers and conferences about communities transformed by the power of Christ. But there are times when we get it wrong in our zeal for God.

Sometimes our message is not about liberation, but about our judgement of the world and the pet sins of the day.

At times, we are so eager that we hurt our brothers and sisters in Christ. Even if we might be right, we are sometimes doing theology in a way that is damaging to others and what we call the voice of love is perceived as condemnation and judgement. Over the last decades, the church has been good at making headlines in the news while the world is marvelling. People hear a lot about what the church is against, especially same-sex marriage and ordination of LGBT+ pastors. The church has also made a lot of noise on issues like abortion, pornography, divorce, remarriage, carnivals, Islam, etc.

Paul is one of the New Testament favourites. His personal writing is extensive, with even the Book of Acts predominantly focusing on his life and ministry. Paul's writing can be quite tough to read as it involves difficult discussions about local issues, and theological hot potatoes of the day. Paul is often loved or loathed.

Paul's outlook on life was very much black and white. His focus changed dramatically, but he was still a man of great passion, and he wore blinkers. Nothing would deter him from his mission. Doesn't it sound like a lot of modern-day management advice: set a goal, plan, stick to the goals, and celebrate your success. Paul was effective possibly because he was well-educated in his field, experienced and intentional. He was invested in his ministry. It was not just a nice thought or a New Year resolution. It was his life. His mission became his life - and he was sold out for God and His cause.

Stephen, too, was on fire for God (6:8). He was commissioned as a deacon with responsibility for organising the distribution of help to the Greek widows in the city. And what a deacon he was. He was full of faith. Power, signs, and wonders flowed from his life. I think many churches need to check their job description for their deacons! New Testament deacons were not just doing practical stuff, they did social action and justice work in the power of God. While Paul was hunting down people, Stephen was liberating immigrant widows from extreme poverty. Both had a passion for God, but one was building up the Kingdom while the other one was tearing it apart. Both thought they were right and that they had God on their side.

Unfortunately, Paul and his band of brothers were having the upper hand and it was costly for Stephen. He was put on trial for his faith and lost the battle, but he gained the Kingdom. During all this unfairness, Stephen was able to practise the presence of God, holding on to the Holy Spirit. He saw the glory of God while facing the ugliness of religious life. He even had a revelation of Jesus being in control at the right hand of our Creator God (7:55). It is amazing to meditate on this short passage about Stephen. The Holy Spirit moulded his life, so he responded like Jesus. He was a true Christian, a little Jesus, while being treated unfairly. He could see into the heavens and was enabled to forgive his opponents and their evil deeds in the name of God (7:56, 60).

What flows out of you and me when we are mistreated? Is the heart of Jesus pouring out, or is it abuse, accusations, and bitterness? When we get a revelation of who God is, and learn to see God in all things, then we can better cope with the realities of an unjust world. We need to keep on seeing Jesus, see what He is up to, see the open heavens, so we can live in the knowledge of a God who is not far away, who is not sending evil our way, but who is with us in the storms of life.

Stephen saw Jesus, while Paul saw his mission. Paul approved of the stoning of a godly man. Stephen was a man serving the poor with food and signs and wonders (8:1). Paul had no problem destroying others, that others were put out of fellowship and taken from their homes, because he had the right interpretation of Scripture. He had a perverted view of God and His mission, but that did not stop him from forcing "acts of God" on other people.

Haven't we heard that a lot in the LGBT+ communities from well-known preachers. We are responsible for all evil, from hurricanes to earthquakes. It amazes me that 2 - 5% of the population who just want to be allowed to love another person without discrimination, can have such a hugely negative impact on society and bring about natural disasters. I thought I was quite an insignificant person, but when it comes to scapegoating, then I am suddenly playing the major leagues. The preaching does not add up to the lifestyle of Jesus, but it is popular with certain groups in society. It seems radical, and it offers a reason for the ills of society. Demonising a small group of people has been a winner throughout history, politically and in faith communities.

Stephen was able to forgive, because he knew that they were sinning against him and the Kingdom, not the other way around (7:60). We need to understand the Spirit of the word or we end up believing many different accusations made against us in the LGBT+ communities. We need to reflect on what it means to miss the mark, to sin, from a Godly point of view.

We can read that God has predestined us to become like Jesus, so anything that stops us from that, is sin. We are called to be followers of Jesus and His way of life. We are called to use the unique abilities that He has given us as well as our spiritual gifts to serve Him and His purposes. Paul wanted to stop Stephen and the church from doing the right thing. By persecuting the believers in Jerusalem, he tried to stop their help to the immigrant widows and other vulnerable people as well as their preaching and exercising the power of the Spirit (8:1).

Looking at Paul's actions in hindsight, it is easy to see that they are anti-Christ, but Stephen knew that while it was going on. He had the spiritual discernment to meet the challenge for what it was. He was being sinned against and he asked God not to judge them for their wrongdoings. What a difference to many of the anti-LGBT preachers, who condemn us to eternal destruction. It is so clear that the Holy Spirit was present in Stephen's life, for he asked God to have mercy on people destroying his life and ministry. There may be things we do not like about others, there may be things we perceive as sin, but we are encouraged to pray for the welfare of others. That is the way of the Kingdom, the way of love, and that love has the potential to transform lives. It is my prayer, that we will remember that no matter which side we are on when it comes to inclusion and affirmation of Christians from the LGBT+ communities.

As Stephen died, faithful people were heartbroken over his death (8:2). We see a great illustration of Christian communities at work. People gathered when others were treated unjustly, and the believers lamented his death. A man of God, a deacon full of faith and power, had been stoned to death for his faith and his service to the poor. He was a martyr and he was not the last one in history. People may lose their lives for doing the right thing. People of faith who use their faith to make a difference are dangerous to the people who benefit from the power structures in our society. Christians are the mustard seed conspiracy, as Dallas Willard calls it. We are the underground movement sowing seeds of liberation and love in worn out communities as well as in the political and financial hotspots around the world. Christians educate people, so they may take steps out of poverty, care for the terminally ill, offer prison teaching and women's empowerment programmes. The church of Christ is moving in where others are moving out. These are signs of people of faith, which will always challenge the status quo, and some will lose money, power, or prestige when the church shows up.

Not only were the people of Israel under Roman oppression, but the new believers also had to face the wrath of Paul (8:3-9:2). He destroyed their faith communities, dragged people off to prison, men and women alike. Nobody was safe. In these situations, it is hard to know what to do, but many people dispersed out of the city and settled throughout the regions of Judah and Samaria (8:1).

Similarly, our teaching and preaching can create havoc in the lives of fellow believers and people listening from the margins. Personally, I know how much the teaching of the church led to self-loathing, body-shaming, and oddly enough the teaching also damaged my faith.

I know that we are saved by grace, but I learnt in the church that grace does not do for gay people. It was clear from the different sermons I listened to. Therefore, I had to do all the works too. Maybe, just maybe it would give me a few brownie points with God. But I also realised that it was bad Christianity. I can never earn my way to God's heart or to the heart of those who hold a classic interpretation of the Bible in relation to LGBT+ communities, same-sex marriage, etc. To them, I am and always will be a lost cause. I will never be good enough.

This teaching has damaged my soul and my thinking, and it is taking time for me to let go of the shame, the guilt, and a damaging view of God as the cosmic terrorist.

We see that Paul's passion for God made him ugly. He was behind awful deeds against humanity. He was behind religious cleansing of a faith community.

It is easy for us to become just as ugly in our fight against the theology that has crushed our souls. It is easy to fight back using the same weapons as those thrown against us.

Many denominations vote about theology. Many of us in the Christian LGBT+ communities follow the debate and the decisions made, but I am not sure that it is the way of the Kingdom.

Stephen did not fight back at Paul. He explained his theological position, but he did not try to create alliances to fight back at Paul and his accomplices.

When it comes to voting in our churches, we just learn who currently hold the majority. The problem is that the majority do not convince the minority. They just won over them and it is splitting denominations and churches.

I hear of worldwide denominations that do not know what to do after decades of discussions about LGBT+, because they know that they can lose churches and members on certain continents if they embrace an inclusive interpretation of the Bible. While they keep on discussing, people are getting hurt. LGBT+ members and pastors are dispersed. Some lose their faith, others become passive, while some join affirming churches and denominations.

Voting creates winners and losers, which is of the world. Personally, I believe that we all need Damascus revelations of Jesus (8:3-5). Paul thought he was right, and he was eager in his mission. He had the right view of God. He had received training from an extremely strict rabbi and was experienced in ministry. No book and no new research would have convinced him about anything different. I think many of us are the same when it comes to certain subjects of theology. We know what we believe, and we are not going to change that view easily. We may study the subject, but we know the answer, so we read all the research with those eyes. Sometimes we even choose the research or the books that suit our preferences. So, like Paul, we need God, we need new revelation for healthy change to take place.

Paul was changed because of Jesus. Paul's destructive mission was closed in an instant. There were no negotiations, new proposals, or amendments. It was all done by the Spirit of God.

How we need the Holy Spirit to help us get a deeper and greater revelation of our Saviour. How we need to keep on being moulded by the Spirit of the Word and not the letter of the Word. How we need to examine ourselves daily and to invite the Spirit to do His work in us, so that we may serve God rather than our mission.

We need people who are on fire for God, the Stephen way. We need people to become Christians like him who focus on forgiveness for wrongdoing, proclaim a liberating Gospel of grace, and who are willing to take the consequences as there is a good chance that they will be persecuted in the process.

So, as a gay man, I have a decision to make. Will I become bitter or better because of what people have done to me? Will I reject the Gospel because I have been hurt by a classic interpretation of the Bible, or will I allow myself to explore what the Jesus Way may look like for me?

I have noticed that many different theologies are popping up these years. Just to mention a few: Feminist, Queer, Dalit, Palestinian, Black, and Liberation theology. It tells me one thing: Our classic interpretation of the Bible has hurt a lot of people around the world, leading to oppression and discrimination. For some it is about life and death. We may look with great dismay at these attempts at finding the good news of the Bible for people who are hurting under the teaching and practices of the church. Some of the attempts might be too radical and too far out, but they are attempts to stay within the faith. I think we should celebrate that.

When, hundreds of years ago, people like Ignatius, Luther and Calvin or movements like the Anabaptists and Quakers preached their new theologies, it created an uproar. People were being killed, sent away from their homes, churches, etc. We have never been good at taking a hard look at our teaching. We are too scared of heresy, even today, to engage in creative and critical thinking, I believe. We create camps and we dig in our heels. This kind of attitude is very much like Paul's, but later he concluded that he counted it all as loss (Philippians 3:7). Some versions say, "dung." A life without Christ is empty. Having a challenging mission is exciting, but it may be the wrong mission that hurts the Body of Christ, the believers, as well as society around us.

I want to have a heart like that of Stephen, so I become like Jesus even in times of crisis. I do not want to destroy lives like Paul, because I just know the right theology. I need to let go of having to win the vote. Instead, let us be transformed by the renewing of our minds. Let us dare to consider what a theology would look like that liberates the oppressed, lifts the underrepresented, and gives hope to the hopeless. Maybe we need a new reformation to identify what the Spirit is saying to the churches today?

Being on Fire for God (Philip)

Acts 8:4-13, 26-30, 35-37, 39-40 (David Bentley Hart Translation)

4 So those who had been scattered went all about, proclaiming the word of the good tidings.

5 And Philip, going down to the city of Samaria, proclaimed the Anointed to them.

6 And, with one accord, the crowds paid attention to what was said by Philip, as they listened to him and saw the signs that he performed.

7 For many of those having impure spirits in them, shouting out in a loud voice, came out; and many who were paralysed and lame were healed,

8 And there was a great deal of rejoicing in that city.

9 Now, previous to this, a certain man by the name of Simon had been practicing magic in the city and astonishing the people of Samaria, presenting himself as someone great,

10 To whom everyone, from small to great, gave heed, saying, "This man is the Power of God, which is called Great."

11 And they have him their attention because, for a considerable time, he had amazed them with his feats of magic,

12 But when they believed Philip, as he proclaimed the good tidings concerning the Kingdom of God and the name of Jesus the Anointed, they were baptised, men and women both.

13 And Simon himself also had faith and having been baptised he attached himself to Philip and, seeing the signs and great feats of power taking place, he was amazed...

26 But an angel of the Lord spoke to Philip, saying, "Arise and go southward on the road leading down from Jerusalem to Gaza." This is wilderness.

27 And, arising, he went. And look: An Ethiopian man, a eunuch – a courtier of Candance, Queen of the Ethiopians, one who was in charge of all her treasury – had gone to Jerusalem to worship,

28 And was returning, and was seated in his chariot and was reading the prophet Isaiah.

29 And the Spirit said to Philip, "Approach this chariot and accompany it."

30 And, running up, Philip heard him reading Isaiah the prophet, and said, "Do you really understand the things you are reading?"...

35 And opening his mouth Philip, beginning with this scripture, announced to him the good tidings of Jesus.

36 And, as they were traveling among the road, they came upon some water, and the eunuch says, "Look, water. What prevents me being baptised?"

37 And Philip said, "It is possible, if you have faith with all your heart." And in reply he said, "I have faith that Jesus the Anointed is God's Son."

39 And when they came up out of the water a Spirit of the Lord seized Philip away, and the eunuch did not see him again, for he went on his way rejoicing.

40 But Philip found himself in Azotus and, passing through it, he proclaimed the good tidings to all the cities, until he came to Caesarea.

As I was studying Paul and the way his passion for God destroyed people's lives, I noticed, that sandwiched between the persecutions and his revelation of Jesus, there were three short stories about Philip. It got me curious, especially when I saw Philip ministering to different groups of people who were misfits in the eyes of the religious establishment. Like Stephen, Philip shows us what being filled with the Holy Spirit looks like, and it is a beautiful picture.

As Paul scattered the believers, we see that this did not stop them from loving and serving God (8:4). They did not need an established mainstream church in order to preach, but rather saw their displacement as an opportunity to reach more people. How easy it is to do the opposite, complaining and asking God where He is hiding in times of trouble. Instead, the early believers did not take persecution and being thrown out of the church as a hindrance, and neither should we.

One of the first things I did on returning to Denmark after losing my position as a pastor, was to find an affirming church. I knew it would be easy to sit back, lick my battle wounds, and get angry with the church. I knew I could quickly become a bad role model to my former church members and others who know me. I needed to find a church, no matter what. I had to find a place where I could fully engage and minister. God opened the doors for that in, as far as I know, the only fully inclusive free church in our capital city. (The Evangelical Lutheran church is the Danish State church; all other denominations are called free churches because they are free of the state.)

I might not be a paid church pastor at the time of writing (2018), but I am able to preach God's Word and teach in different settings. In the spirit of this text, it is important for us in the LGBT+ communities not to give up, but to keep on serving God actively and passionately even when we are sent away. Let us start new (house) churches and ministries if we are not fully welcome where we are. The gospel is too important for us to become lukewarm or to just sit passively in the pews and pay our tithes.

The gospel was so important to Philip that he refused to let people like Paul decide what he could or could not do. We can see that he made some radical choices that show us the heart of God in action. A loving God inspires us to make radical choices, and Philip was led to the down-and-out of his day.

Philip first went to the Samaritans (8:5). The Samaritans were hated for historical reasons, being of mixed race and not following the Jewish faith in the correct way. Philip did not care about the rules, the culture, or the traditions. He went straight to this region, and with great results. First, he focused on the culturally and socially excluded.

Philip did not dilute the Gospel or downplay the miracles, rather he showed what is possible in the power of the Holy Spirit. He communicated the Gospel and performed miracles (8:6). He was not intimidated by Paul and his allies, even though they might hear about him and what he was up to when engaging in such a public ministry. News travelled fast even in an age without mobiles, Skype or Facebook. People were so poor and often ill that they would do anything to be able to listen to a liberator and a faith healer.

I have noticed that some LGBT+ Christians have almost rejected the Bible because of the pain they have experienced through classic interpretations of the Bible. Philip did not let Paul's interpretation, misuse and abuse stop him from passing on as much good news as possible. This happened through preaching and deliverance (8:7). The people of Samaria were set free from unclean spirits as well as paralysis and other ailments. People were reached and rejoiced because Philip refused to slow down or go dark to protect himself (8:8). He did not let his own pain stop him from passing on God's loving grace to others, especially to those who were perceived as bad company.

As part of ministering to the Samaritans, Philip came across Simon who dabbled in the supernatural (8:9-10). Today, we may think of some New Age practices, or people practising the supernatural from other faith traditions. We may say that he was spiritual, but not doctrinal.

Simon got interested in Philip, his message, and power. Philip was not intimidated by Simon's display of power but felt safe in his own faith in God and the workings of the Holy Spirit. I have noticed that some within our LGBT+ communities become more interested in other religions or alternative spiritual practices because their own Christian tradition has been toxic to their well-being.

Philip shows us that it is possible not to throw the baby out with the bath water, but to hold on to what is good, trusting Christ who has the power to transform lives, heal the broken-hearted, and deliver us from evil.

These years, there is a political debate in several countries. How can we define what it means to be Danish, English, American, Polish, etc.? Some governments publish canons of literature, values, etc. to define their own people group. I read some research showing that many people in Denmark find that Muslims do not fit into Danish society, because they do not share our cultural heritage. They are not real Danes no matter how integrated they are!

At the same time, a large majority of Danes do not engage in the Christian faith, yet they feel threatened by people of other faith traditions. Philip did the opposite. He was not scared by Simon's spiritual practices, he just showed people like Simon what Jesus can do. This impressed Simon so much that he believed and was baptised.

Instead of being afraid of the other or rejecting his Christian faith tradition because it has hurt him, Philip showed us in the LGBT+ communities that we can embrace our Christian faith, hold on to Christ who sets people free. Philip focused on the Good News in his preaching and through healing and deliverance. As a result, people embraced the faith and were baptised (8:12)

During this visit to Samaria, Philip received a word of knowledge about going south (8:26). He did not dismiss it as a crazy thought but tested if it was from God by going. How often do we receive hints from Heaven and maybe dismiss them, because it is inconvenient or because we do not habitually listen to the voice of God?

Philip went and encountered yet another misfit. This time it was a foreigner from Egypt, but there was an added twist. He was not an ordinary man: He was a eunuch (8:27).

We are not used to eunuchs in the Western world, so it does not necessarily ring a bell when we read it. We are used to the binary model of male or female from the creation story. Notice that Jesus rejected this concept by adding a third gender or three kinds of eunuchs to the mix (Matthew 19:12). There are those who were born castrated or with a birth defect, disease, or mutilation. Then there were the people who were castrated by others (sinned against?) and those who chose to become eunuchs to serve the Kingdom more efficiently. Some eunuchs were castrated at a young age, which made them very attractive as they were men by birth but with female features due to the lack of testosterone in the formative years. For some, it meant that they were used for sexual pleasures of others and therefore sinned against even more.

God sent Philip to a region, to an ethnic and religious group that was disliked, then to a man interested in the supernatural, and finally to a sexual minority. What is going on here? Paul was dismissing people and destroying the churches left, right and centre, because he wanted his holiness code to be the only way into the Kingdom of God, but at the same time God and Philip were busy welcoming the people that Paul rejected.

It is interesting to notice, how God was doing all the "wrong things," as Philip made himself available, being led by the Spirit in the middle of his own trauma as a displaced person.

The eunuchs were not welcome at the Temple. They could not join in worship, but God knew the eunuch's heart (8:30). He had gone up to Jerusalem to worship even though he could not join the others. He read the Scriptures but did not understand their spiritual significance. He was hungry for God, but he did not fit the categories of those welcome in the House of God.

Philip did not put up any boundaries for the eunuch but helped him to understand God. There was Good News available even for a eunuch, a sexual minority (8:35). The eunuch could not change his status, orientation, or his lifestyle; he would always be a castrated man, a third gender. There was no lifestyle to lay aside, his body and his orientation would never change. But the eunuch and Philip agreed that he was ready to be baptised into the mystical Body of Christ (8:36-37). He had been excluded from the fellowship of believers, but Philip invited him to join the new community of saints. He was no longer a misfit, he was no longer a deviant, or a sexual minority unfit for salvation. God had led Philip to this man. God was making a point of inclusion in all three instances. Religious people like Paul may be powerful, but God wins in the end.

Paul believed that only Jews and people with certain beliefs and spiritual practices could worship God. Everybody else had to be discouraged by threats, displacements, and imprisonment. Today, the LGBT+ communities are also often being threatened through verbal abuse, being outed and ousted by the church, and in some countries, we are also facing prison or death.

We need to embrace the Good News like Philip. He listened to the Spirit, was led by the Spirit, preached in the power of the Spirit, and ministered in the Spirit, and people rejoiced. The outsiders had become insiders because of God's amazing grace and love. Philip made himself available during a time of personal challenges, and God used him to make a real difference in the lives of individual people as well as in different communities. Let us not overlook the significance of God pursuing a person from a sexual minority so he could join the family of God. He was not a second-rate Christian with certain limitations. He became a full member because there are only full members in the Body of Christ. We are the priesthood of all believers. In the Kingdom of Heaven there is no ranking, no status, only a call to serve others and God.

When Philip had sent the eunuch on his way, the Spirit led him to minister in other cities. His ministry of the Word was not over. It had just begun, and the negative voices and threats did not stop him from doing good. Other people's lives depended on him, just as other people's lives, faith, and liberation depend on us.

Wheat or Weird?

Matthew 13:24-30 (David Bentley Hart Translation)

24 He set another before them saying, "The Kingdom of the heavens has been likened to a man sowing good seed in his field.

25 But, when men were asleep, his enemy came and sowed darnel-seeds as well, in among the grain, and departed.

26 And when the crop sprouted and bore fruit the darnel-weeds also appeared.

27 And the householder's slaves, approaching, said to him, "Lord, did you not sow good seed in your field? Where have the darnel-weeds it contains come from?"

28 And he said to them, "Someone who is an enemy did this." So the slaves say to him, "Do you wish then that we should go out and gather them?"

29 But he says, "No, lest in gathering the darnel-weeds you should uproot the grain along with them.

30 Let them both grow up together until the harvest; and at the time of the harvest I shall tell the reapers, "First gather the darnel-weeds and tie them in sheaves in order to burn them; but gather the grain into my granary." ""

Mark 4:28 (David Bentley Hart Translation)

The earth bears fruit of itself, first a shoot, then an ear, then the full grain within the ear.

WHAT WILL BE the end product, the fruit of your life? When you started out did you have a game plan in mind? Did you know where you would be decades later?

I wonder if we sometimes judge others before they even get a chance to grow and develop. Sometimes we may fear people and cultures just because they seem strange to us. Diversity sounds nice in theory, but it is scary and messy. I want more people to be like me, to believe like me, and to act like me, then I can read the situation. I am at ease in such situations, but the world is getting more complicated as we travel more extensively, with greater levels of migration, and we see news stories on the TV that we would never hear about in the past.

With social media we all have a platform to share our views. There is no filter, so we get bombarded with messages and conflicting messages. Therefore, some of us end up primarily having likeminded people as friends also on social media, since having to cope with otherness is too taxing. The political and church discourse gets to be about 'us and them' instead of 'what do we have in common'.

We may be eager to stay faithful to our understanding of the Bible and to our faith tradition. We know we shouldn't judge a book by its cover; but judging comes easy to us as we have learnt what to think: We do not like the Catholics because they pray in front of icons, we do not like the Pentecostals because they speak in tongues, we do not like the Baptists because they are liberals, we do not like the Mennonites because they are old fashioned, we do not like the Orthodox because they pray set prayers, we do not like the Adventists because they are vegetarians and worship on a Saturday. We do not like the new church streams because they have stepped out of the mainstream. We do not like the gays because they challenge our understanding of sexual orientation and gender identity.

Richard Rohr writes that Christian maturity is a bit like the three sections of the Old Testament. At first, you become very binary. Things are either black or white, true or false. Spiritual discernment is easy, you are either in or out. This is like the historical books of the Old Testament.

If you go to the next stage of faith, you become like the prophets who challenged the status quo, the abuse, the unhelpful traditions, and classical ways of looking at things. Spiritual discernment is also quite easy at this stage, as you mainly oppose what other people are doing and believing.

At the third stage of spiritual maturity you learn to live with paradoxes as seen in the wisdom books of the Old Testament. You allow for all the human emotions, you see many shades of grey, and juggle complexity. You may come to different conclusions at different times.

I like his understanding of spiritual maturity, and I can see how easy it is for us to train our church members to stay at the first level. We quote a verse and that is how the cookie crumbles. There is no discussion, that is just how it is. It is easy to be a zealot at this stage because Christian spirituality is straight forward. Whatever you do is either sinful or holy and we follow a certain code of holiness that we expect everybody else to abide by.

Coming back to a Kingdom focus and allowing for complexity, may help us in our Christian walk, but it is tough, and it does not look that spiritual at first.

Jesus told people about the sower. The believer sowing the good stuff expected a fruitful return (13:24). I see that in my own life. I long to make a difference. I long to see that something good comes out of all the long hours in ministry, in prayer, in preparing the next sermon, and when serving food for the migrants and the homeless. I want something good to come out of my dedication.

Many people in Denmark do not perceive my work among the migrants as good work. Politically, a high percentage of the population are against migrants, they are against the poor coming from Eastern Europe to collect bottles to earn money for their families. So, when we create a safe space for them, a place to get a hot meal, some clothes, and a chance to talk to a health professional, then some people think we are doing a harmful job. One official told me that if we do a good job, then we might see more migrants in the country and that is not a preferable outcome. So how do I know if I am planting good seeds or bad seeds? The public opinion is unhelpful as a measuring rod.

We hear that beggars and people sleeping rough are making other people feel unsafe on television and in the newspapers. In my mind that is weed thinking (13:25). I cannot fathom that we as a rich society put up barriers for the poor who try to support their loved ones by collecting bottles. Wouldn't we do the same if we were in the same position?

The amount of money sent home from migrants and immigrants to their poor families is much higher than the foreign aid paid by governments. Some politicians state that it must pay to work, but when people are working instead of just living off benefits, then we say it is wrong. How am I to know if I am in the will of God? Am I wheat or weird when I think like this? According to common public opinion I am damaging society and weed is the fruit of my life. How to discern what is good and what is bad?

As a result of what we plant – our behaviour, and what we say – we reap some results, but in the beginning, they are just sprouts (13:26). In the UK after the Brexit referendum, there was an increase in hate crimes. Was that related? Was that a consequence of a negative campaign? We do not know for sure at first. It takes time to discern what is really going on.

We hear of statistics indicating that more LGBT+ Christians are committing suicide compared to LGBT+ people without a Christian faith. Is that the result of Christian teaching or is it rooted in something else? We see a trend, but where does it take us?

We may be able to guess what is to come when we look at new situations, but how to be sure? Disruption, frustration, and confusion may follow people who are different. We notice the tension, but how do we know if they represent something that is good or bad.

Jesus is telling us that there are barriers to the gospel (13:28). There is a real enemy, the spirit of the Antichrist, who is sowing weeds that strangle a life-giving, liberating, and true faith, so I am called to discern. I am thinking of Peter who got it so right and so wrong within minutes: He proclaimed that Jesus was the Christ, which was a true revelation from God. He had understood the nature of Jesus. Afterwards Jesus said that He had to go away to be killed and Peter got upset as he wanted to hold on to his friend. Peter wanted Jesus to choose Easy Street, instead of the cross. Peter in his love for Christ, became a mouthpiece of the Devil. Our longings can make us do God's will or the will of the opposer.

Paul was a man of zeal. He persecuted the Christians and approved of people getting killed for their faith. He had a single-minded focus. He was serving God, but he was doing the Devil's business. He knew Scripture well, but he did not understand the God of Scripture. He could quote and debate, but he did not see Jesus and the ways of the Kingdom, so he hurt a lot of people.

Sometimes we need to let things emerge to see clearly. The story tells us that we may damage a lot of people if we act too quickly (13:29). Uprooting everything that looks different can be harmful.

Since Emperor Constantine, the church has often turned to rules and regulations. We have made decisions of who is in and who is out. Under Constantine the bishops would decide and then the army would enforce their decisions. The oppressed became the oppressors. There was only one way of looking at the Christian faith, and all other traditions and interpretations were banned.

Later in history we had the inquisition and the reformation when we again made rules for who would be acceptable to the church. Those who did not conform, who did not fall in line with the flavour of the month, experienced the wrath of the church.

Jesus challenged us to allow things to grow, so we may discern. He said that if we uproot everything that behaves different at the initial stage then we will also end up uprooting all the good stuff. In our desire to please God and his people, we hurt His church and His family.

We have been there before. We were told it would be the end of the world if women could become church leaders, instead female pastors, missionaries, and bishops added something to the church. We were told that the church would be corrupted by immorality; but having divorced and remarried pastors has not meant the end to Christianity as we know it.

Throughout the world churches are being divided over gay marriage. The debate is fierce and it easy for us to end up taking a defensive position no matter our theological perspective and political views. We do not want to get hurt, so we protect ourselves as we bunch together in our holy huddles of likeminded people.

LGBT+ Christians like myself have been forced out of church and I have been told that I will now lose my faith or become a liberal (remember that is a very bad word in certain Christian circles). How do they know? When some Christians hear that I have come out they make conclusions immediately as their minds have been made up. Being gay means that I cannot be a good seed. What if their storyline is not my storyline? What if there is no blueprint for LGBT+ people? How will we know, when churches are closing their doors to the ministry of LGBT+ Christian people like me? We do not allow for the sprout to grow so we can discern if it is good or bad.

At the same time, there is confusion in the camp, because I still choose church. I still write Christian books. I love to preach, teach, prophesy, and serve the poor. I do not fit the stereotype that we hear from certain pulpits, but I must be bad and deceived because that fits the narrative.

Jesus is asking us to withhold our judgements and to allow things to grow. He even allowed Judas to be close to Him, to hold a power ministry, and be His ministry companion onto the end of Judas's life. Jesus was not afraid of his disciples and He did not push them away even when he did not like all their actions. Jesus kept on calling people into fellowship not conformity.

The earth bears fruit by itself because that is the way God created the universe (Mark 4:28). You plant something and it will grow and only as it grows will we be able to discern if that is a healthy or an unhealthy lifestyle. All our small decisions take us either closer to or away from Jesus. That is why we need discernment. Even ministry can take us away from Jesus, making us so busy that we do not have time for the relationship and the friendship with our Saviour and our families. There are no guarantees so therefore we must wait and see. That is the Way of the Kingdom and God is patient.

Gamaliel offered great advice and I wish we would all take it to heart, when we experience some of the weird and wonderful in the world of faith.

> *Acts 5:38-39* (David Bentley Hart Translation)
>
> *(Gamaliel:) 38 And now I say to you, stand back from these men and leave them; for if this movement or this work is from men it will be destroyed;*
>
> *39 But if it is from God you will not be able to destroy them; you might even turn out to be men who are battling against God.*

We send LGBT+ Christians packing who are trying to follow Christ and live with integrity, integrated and with authenticity, because we do not agree with their Bible interpretation.

We do not allow for Christian LGBT+ role models/pastors/leaders to develop, so we can discern if they are honouring God or not.

So, am I a good seed or am I a weed? Am I ready for salvation or damnation? Jesus says, wait and see.

Can a glitter gay, a vanilla gay, a sexually active or a celibate gay enter the Kingdom of God? Jesus says, wait and see. His litmus test will focus on our love for God and humankind.

Off Script

Luke 7:36-50 (David Bentley Hart Translation)

36 Now a certain one of the Pharisees requested him to dine with him; and entering the Pharisee's house he reclined at the table.

37 And look: There was a woman in the city who was a sinner, and knowing that he is reclining in the home of the Pharisee, and bringing an alabaster phial of unguent,

38 And standing behind, weeping at his feet, she began to make his feet wet with her tears, and she wiped them off with the hair of her head, and fervently kissed his feet and anointed them with unguent.

39 But, seeing this, the Pharisee who had invited him talked to himself, saying, "This man, if he were a prophet, would have known who and of what sort this woman who touches him is, for she is a sinner."

40 And in reply Jesus said to him, "Simon, I have something to say to you." And he says, "Speak, teacher."

41 There were two men indebted to a certain moneylender: The one owed five hundred denarii and the other fifty.

42 As they had nothing with which to replay, he graciously forgave them both. Which of them, therefore, will love him more?"

43 In reply Simon said: "The one to whom he freely forgave more." And he said to him, "You have judged correctly."

44 And turning to the woman he said to Simon, "Do you see this woman? I entered your home, you did not give me water for my feet; but she washed my feet with her tears and wiped them off with her hair.

45 You gave me no kiss of friendship, but she from the time I entered has not ceased fervently kissing my feet.

46 You did not anoint my head with oil; but she anointed my feet with unguent.

47 By virtue of which, I tell you her sins – which are many – have been forgiven, because she loved much; but one to whom little is forgiven loves little."

48 And he said to her, "Your sins have been forgiven."

49 And those reclining at table with him began to say among themselves, "Who is this, who even forgives sins?"

50 And he said to the woman, "Your faith has saved you; go in peace."

I THINK THAT SOME people get confused when they think of the LGBT+ communities, as we do not always behave as people expect. When people do not follow the norms of the (church) culture, then they are more difficult to assess. Who are they and what are they all about?

Jesus faced this challenge all the time. He was the Messiah, the chosen One, but He did not behave in the way that people had in mind. He was no king like David or military commander like Joshua. He was Himself and He was different. Jesus kept on messing with people's minds about God, faith, and behaviour. He chose grace over justice; He rebuked the insiders and forgave the outsiders. They were not able to predict just how far He would go, so the religious leaders tried to trap Him.

I read a note on Facebook after Copenhagen Pride. The person asked what it was all about. I noticed some people saying that they really did not like what was going on, but they had not been around to see the Parade. Within the LGBT+ communities I have heard it discussed if we have become too vanilla and have lost our edge. What a difference in opinion. When people argue against Pride I often feel like saying, tongue in cheek, that I do not like all the hetero parties either. You know, the music festivals that are all about "Sex, drugs and rock 'n' roll." Why do straight people have such a need to misbehave and show off their sexuality? Just asking...

It is funny how certain behaviours by some people are acceptable, while other people's behaviours are so off-putting? Maybe it is a stress reaction because we are not sure how to read and handle situations when people go off script and we see and hear things we are not used to.

In this passage, two people went off script, but Jesus was spiritually in control of the situation, so God was glorified through it all.

A bold woman came to the house while Jesus was having His dinner (7:37-38). She did not take over in any way. She was very quiet, actually. She just stood there behind Jesus, her tears flowing down onto his feet. She began to wipe His feet and kiss them. What an act of love. The woman even anointed His feet. I am reminded of the Old Testament where they anointed kings, priests, and prophets. Here it was a sinful woman who took upon herself the role of a prophet, as she had a sense of who Jesus was, and she anointed Him for ministry. How powerful that the down and outs, in the view of society, are those who understood Jesus and who were not afraid of showing it.

The woman came to Jesus, not as a successful and respected woman, but she came to Him with her broken heart. She was not afraid of showing remorse and affection towards Jesus. She did what many people find difficult to do. Approaching Jesus without all the religious pomp and circumstance. Instead, she came vulnerable to Jesus. She knew she did not have any claim to fame or to be seen or heard. She just wanted to surrender her life to Jesus.

The situation did not look good. She entered the house of a religious person, and I can only guess what people might think when a religious outsider, a sinner, approached and touched the guest of honour. She did not follow the etiquette. Maybe she did not know the script, because normally she would have no opportunity to approach God. The religious people stood in her way. Who cares about a sinner, and a woman anyway?

It is amazing how quickly we can judge a situation and how wrong we can be. The Pharisee got upset with Jesus, because a true prophet would know that he should have nothing to do with such a woman (7:39). The woman did not fit into his holiness code and what to expect from such a gathering. She had no place at the table because he thought that it was reserved to the important people like himself.

I can think of so many situations, where I am told directly or indirectly that I am not welcome at the table as a gay man. I do not fit in and we do not like a messy church. Once I was put forward by a friend for a position as a pastor. I told him that I was sure that it would not lead to anything, but he wanted to try anyway. Shortly afterwards he called me to say that he had been told that no congregation within that denomination would have anything to do with me. We did not even get to discuss celibacy, same-sex marriage, or relationships. Just being gay was a step too far. I would not be invited to the party. I could not serve, because being gay and Christian was an oxymoron in their minds: "Gay Christians are depraved and deceived." I thought we were going to be judged by the fruits of our lives, as bad trees cannot produce good fruit! I guess this is yet another of the Biblical sayings that for some reason do not apply to us.

Jesus had a different kind of worshippers surrounding Him and He did not have any issue with that. Just as this woman was met with suspicion, so are we. I am learning that I need to go to Jesus, not to the church, with all my brokenness. It is my responsibility to take steps closer to Jesus even when a crowd of religious leaders are in my way. church culture and nationalism should never stop us from following Jesus.

Jesus challenged Simon the Pharisee (7:40-42). He did not allow him to get away with his judgemental thoughts, so Jesus talked about love, debt, and forgiveness. And guess what, love always wins. Not because love is easy, or love is blind, but because God is love. This love coped with our wrath on the cross and Jesus still forgave us. It was not cheap nor easy.

The love of God shows itself as compassion for people who are desperate for change. Just as the woman showed love in action as she anointed and wiped the feet of Jesus, so Jesus showed love in action by living, dying, returning to life and sending his Holy Spirit to us to empower us and liberate us. Love is the only thing that can change hearts and it is never cheap.

Simon followed Jesus's storyline and answered what was expected of him (7:42). There is a link between love and forgiveness. We do not love God because we are afraid of hell. We love God because of His loving grace. He embraced us while we were still sinners and messed around. He still loves us when we mess around today. We can love because He is love.

The Pharisee wanted a guest of honour in his home, but Jesus noticed who was the real follower at the party (7:44). Simon did not do the ordinary things expected of a good host, but the woman who was not welcome went far and beyond what was expected of any host. She had come to surrender. She brought her authentic self to the situation. She did not pretend to be somebody else.

I am reminded of a story told by Tony Campolo in his book, "Speaking my mind." He refers to a conversation with one of his pastor friends in Brooklyn. The pastor had accepted to officiate at a funeral for a man who had died from AIDS, as no other minister wanted to do it.

Campolo described how his friend came to the funeral home, 25 - 30 gay men sat there as if they were frozen in their chairs. He read a few Scriptures, made some general remarks as he did not know the person and he ended the service quickly. People showed no emotion.

They went to the cemetery where he conducted the funeral, and no-body said a thing. Everybody was just motionless as they stood by the grave. He said the benediction and wanted to leave. As the funeral party did not move, he asked them if there was something, he could do for them.

One person said that he had hoped to hear Psalm 23 read aloud as he really liked that Psalm. He then read the Psalm to them. Thereafter, another person requested that he read the passage from Romans that nothing can separate us from the love of God. When he read this passage, he noticed signs of emotion for the first time in their faces. Then one by one they made requests of having scripture read to them for almost an hour!

How easily we get people wrong. Real followers come in all shapes and sizes, they can be glitter gays or vanilla gays, but that tells you nothing about their love for God. The church has forgotten that, so we need to push our way towards Jesus, so we can worship and hear

His voice. The Pharisee had forgotten what faith looks like, so he did not look at the heart, but he looked at the outward appearance.

Recently, I organised a dinner for 40 of our homeless and migrants. I had asked two people to come and sing and play some gospel songs. As they were singing and playing, I noticed how different people were touched at different times. After a few songs, I noticed how some of the Africans became very silent and touched by the lyrics about God's love and protection. Then the Spirit moved to the Romanians and then from table to table, nation group after nation group. God reminded hungry and homeless people from different nations about His love and protection for them and for their families. He was there in their pain and suffering just like He was there at the funeral party and the woman in the passage.

Jesus made His point: The woman was changed because of her love and her faith. The love and faith that had led her to gate crash the dinner party, that had led her to stand in the background crying over Jesus's feet, that had made her dry His feet and anoint Him. Love and faith moved her into action because our inner reality affects our behaviour.

We learn that her love for Jesus led to her being forgiven for her wrongdoings (7:47). We learn that her faith saved her, so she could now leave the party at peace (7:49). Jesus went off script. He should have sent her away as she was a sinner. He should have focused on the religious leaders and the important host as was expected of Him. Instead He used the situation to show God's inclusiveness. He looked for love and faith and found it in the woman and not among the religious leaders. The verse can also be translated that her faith had healed or rescued her. Transformation, deep transformation had taken place in her heart, therefore she did not conform, but she dared to love extravagantly.

We can get healed from our self-hatred, our shame, and the traumatic experiences that may have affected our lives. We can return to everyday life just like the women with peace of mind and wholeness. When we approach Jesus with love and faith, then we can experience a new level of integration because of Him. Surrender always leads us somewhere and following Jesus leads to liberation and wholeness. So, let us push through all the Bible bashing, the proof texting, the clobber passages, the condemning posters at Pride, the discrimination, and let us find our true home in Jesus.

Jesus is not afraid of people who go off script, for it is the (only?) way to do life. It is not a Jesus-centred faith to pretend to be somebody or something that we are not, and it mocks our Maker.

Pause. Breathe. Relax

Psalm 3 (The Passion Translation)

1 Lord, I have so many enemies, so many who are against me.

2 Listen to how they whisper their slander against me, saying: "Look! He's hopeless! Even God can't save him from this!"

Pause in his presence

3 But in the depths of my heart I truly know that you have become my Shield; You take me and surround me with yourself. Your glory covers me continually. You alone restore my courage; for you lift high my head when I bow low in shame.

4 I have cried out to you and from your holy presence. You send me a Father's help.

5 So now I'll lie down and go to sleep – and I'll awake in safety for you surround me with your glory.

6 Even though dark power prowl around me, with their words like sharp arrows, I won't be afraid.

7 I simply cry out to you: "Rise up and help me, Lord! Come and save me!" And you will slap them in the face, breaking the power of their words to harm me.

8 My true Hero comes to my rescue, for the Lord alone is my Saviour. What a feat of favour and bliss he gives his people!

Pause in his presence

I HAD A BAD dream last night. It surprised me a lot as I had just had a wonderful weekend full of celebrations. At 00.41am I woke up. I felt horrible, as a person had tried to kill me in the dream. I did not know the person and I did not know why, but it happened after I had preached a sermon with great boldness in the dream.

In the dream, things were moving on in the church. More people attended the church, and different groups came to the church to do varied things. I had been busy because of the many people coming and going, so I was a bit late for the worship service. I was going to preach, but people sat with their arms crossed and communicated through their body language that they were not happy.

I felt so challenged, so I improvised a sermon where I strongly encouraged people to get in line with God and the move of God's Spirit. How dare we be upset when the church is growing. In my dream, I said it was hypocritical to be upset with growth when we wanted people to come to the Lord.

Right after that, I was in the backseat of a car. A friend was going to drive, but a man stuck his head through the window and tried to kill us with a huge knife. As this was happening, I started to cry out to Jesus in my dream. I called upon His name, I cried out for his protection. At that time, I was entering the phase between being asleep and waking up. I felt paralysed, and I did not wake up, I could only depend on Jesus during this time. Finally, I woke up.

Oddly enough, I was not afraid when I woke up. I was not covered in sweat and my heart was not racing, but I continued to proclaim Jesus, the blood of Jesus, the character of Jesus, and then I started to read aloud the Psalms one by one starting with Psalm 1.

Rather quickly, I got to this Psalm. A Psalm about fighting off evil, having to cope with slandering voices and hate speech (3:1-2). I recognised the feeling. The feeling of having these faceless enemies who stop me from fully entering my calling. The church structures that work against even having respectful discussions about what it means to be a person of faith and LGBT+.

Just today, I read an article about a church in Auburn, Indiana, USA, that had put this text on their church sign: "LGBTQ is a hate crime against God repent." How can anybody be open and transparent about anything deeply personal in that church, and what is it saying to our young people and especially those who have the feeling that they might not fully fit in to our straight society, but they do not know why yet?

There are enemies of open, honest discussions. There are structures that stop us from finding ways to agree to disagree on subject matters that may or may not be clear from the Bible texts. Some of these voices have played on my mind for all too long. They have had all too big a sway over my thoughts, my emotions, and my decision making. I have been held hostage by a system that did not always allow for a rethinking of classic interpretations of the Bible. It is time to break out of the Matrix.

Recently, we celebrated the 500 years of the Lutheran Reformation in Denmark. We appreciated that there were free thinkers who dared to challenge the status quo and the practice and teaching of the established church. The Reformation came with a cost. People were being excommunicated from the church, which was a big thing, some were killed, and many had to flee. Today, we sit back wondering what the fuss was all about. Why did they behave in such a manner? But maybe we are learning that institutions find it hard to change: We read about institutional racism, sexism, homophobia, etc. In our zeal to belong to the right faith and have the right faith, we institutionalise the faith, we take it captive, and we kill off dialogue, make enemies out of our friends and spiritual siblings.

Fear has always been a close and unwelcome companion in my life. Fear of being outed, fear of sickness (HIV as well), fear of dying, fear of losing friends if they truly knew me, and a fear of God. Some enemies were the institutions that ought to protect me, others were cultures that do not allow for diversity, but there were also spiritual leaders and teachers who twisted my thinking, so I could not feel safe with God (3:1).

So where do I go from here? What do I do with the dreams of my youth, where people were out to get me (3:2)? What is it in my life that is so evil that God cannot even save me or want to save me? I was told that falling in love and acting upon it would be a deadly sin. I believed it. Something evil had taken over my life and my sexual orientation would send me to everlasting suffering. I felt hopeless. I could only try to follow God the best I could, but I knew it would never be enough. I knew that others were saved by grace, but not so, when you are gay. Then it is all about a distorted love, a deception, and *the* act. I was told that gay men can never love, only lust after other men!

I can understand why the author of this Psalm wrote, Sala, because it is truly time to pause in God's presence. This life is too hard to live and there is no real way out. For many of us, gay conversation therapy does not work. We may change our sexual behaviour, but that does not change our orientation, attraction, and our longing. We become actors in the great church play, where the top performer is the person who can best conform to the expectations of the church culture.

Pause. Breathe. Relax. Sala.

Deep within I knew that God was different. God had revealed that to me a long time ago (3:3). In 2009 I was ministering in Cuba. I was sitting in a Methodist house church and I had a vision. I saw a court case being played out. I was in the dock. There were lots of people shouting accusations at me, but then Jesus took the stand. He defended me, He stood up for me. He was my shield. People would say all kinds of true or untrue things about me, but I was defended by Jesus. Later in the vision, Jesus and I were dancing. I started hitting Him on His chest out of frustration. I did not want to accept His embrace as I felt life was so unfair. I hit Him, and hit Him repeatedly, but Jesus took it. He could cope with my frustration and fear in the same way as He could cope with all the accusations against me. At last, I could not fight Him anymore and I allowed Him to hold me in His arms as we danced. I was safe at last. I understood that I was loved.

Through revelation I got to know a God whose glory would cover me, but I did not hold on to it. I was ashamed of not being able to live up to the expectations of the church, and I believed they were the expectations of Jesus. He touched me and I was no longer ashamed of being me. Unfortunately, I lost that trust in Him again. Reality hit all too quickly, and I lost the life changing revelation of a God who is my public defender, who is my peace, and who is melting away the shame that had crippled my feeling of self-worth. In God I can find courage to face the visible and invisible enemies of me, my calling, and my faith in Christ.

The cry for help has continued for many years (3:4). Some of these cries have been prayers, but others have come out through all the strong emotions and longings. As I grew older, it became more and more difficult to keep my longings under wraps. I could not control them, they wanted out. My passion for equality grew, my heart for sexual minorities developed, and my longing for a husband consumed me. The Almighty God calmed me through my loving family and affectionate friends. I got a taste for what life could be. It was eye opening, yet frustrating, but I think the Divine parent was leading me.

After praying in my dream, praying out loud as I woke up, and praying Scripture, I was ready to sleep, and I slept like a baby (3:5). The Psalmist was right. It is possible to lie down and feel safe because God is with me. I think this is quite a new experience for me. Normally, after a nightmare, I find it difficult to trust God's presence and his protection. Last night was different as I trusted Him who sets me free. I trusted God to look after me as He did in the awful dream. His glory is all around me because I am grafted into His reality.

I might be caught in the middle of a spiritual battle as we often are (3:6). Life is not always easy in this world, being a world that is in the hands of the evil one as Jesus said (John 12:31). There are battles we win and battles we lose, but I am starting to know that Jesus does not want us to be afraid during these battles.

I am learning to take steps towards trusting Jesus. I have been a Christian for 36 years as I write this (2018), but I have never fully trusted God. How could I, knowing that He would eventually throw me into eternal darkness. My experience also told me that He often would not come through for me. I was obviously such a bad person, so depraved and "*hopeless! Even God can't save him from this*" (3:2).

But my relationship with Jesus, the epiphanies, the words of knowledge and Scripture are changing my mind. Jesus is doing His life transforming work in my heart, mind, psyche, physical body, and my relationships. I react less to the sharp arrows of rejection and unhelpful comments (4:6). I can experience a nightmare where a person wants to kill me, and not be afraid to go to sleep again. That is a huge change for me. I am entering a new reality where God's word and promises are internalised.

With the Psalmist, I can cry out to God to help me, to save me, and to protect me (3:7-8). I no longer try to convince Him to be my God and to look after me. Now, I know it is all about grace and grace will lead me home. It is His grace that comes to my rescue, it is His love that lifts me up. There is nothing I can do to push away His loving kindness, not even being gay or being in a relationship. God alone is my Saviour from myself and the harmful words and actions that I have experienced. Jesus is my hero as He liberated me from my thinking and a theology that was hurting me and my faith.

I do not have to be afraid of the future, of growing old. God is there for me, because He loves His creation, His children. Jesus is the one like the public defender in my vision who will break the power of the harmful words spoken over me, over us. That is worth celebrating. Let the party begin.

Now: Pause. Breathe. Relax. Sala.

My True North

Genesis 22:1-13 (The Orthodox Study Bible)

1 Now it came to pass after these things that God tested Abraham and said to him. "Abraham! Abraham!" And he said, "Here I am."

2 Then He said, "Take now your beloved son, Isaac, whom you love, and go to the land of Moriah, and offer him there as a whole burnt offering on one of the mountains I tell you."

3 So Abraham rose early in the morning and saddled his donkey; and took two of his young men with him, and Isaac his son; and he split firewood for the whole burnt offering, and arose and went to the place God told him.

4 Then on the third day Abraham lifted his eyes and saw the place afar off.

5 Thus Abraham said to his young men, "Stay here with the donkey; the lad and I will go yonder and worship, and we will come back to you."

6 So Abraham took the firewood of the whole burnt offering and laid it on Isaac his son. Then he took the fire in his hand, and a knife, and the two of them went together.

7 Then Isaac spoke to Abraham his father and said, "My father." And he said, "Here I am, my son." Then he said, "Look, the fire and the firewood, but where is the sheep for a whole burnt offering?"

8 And Abraham said, "My son, God will provide for Himself the sheep for a whole burnt offering." So the two of them went together.

9 They came to the place where God had told him. And Abraham built an alter there and placed the firewood in order; and he bound Isaac his son hand and foot and laid him on the alter, upon the firewood.

10 Then Abraham stretched out his hand and took the knife to slay his son.

11 But the Angel of the Lord called to him from heaven and said, "Abraham! Abraham!" So he said, "Here I am."

12 He then replied, "Do not lay your hand on the lad, or do anything to him, for now I know you fear God, since for My sake you have not spared your beloved son."

13 Then Abraham lifted his eyes and looked, and there behind him a ram was caught in a thicket by its horns. So he brought it for a whole burnt offering in the place of his son.

How do we discern what is going on? Life is sometimes a bit complicated. On one hand, Abraham had a son at last, and on the other, God asked him to sacrifice him.

Like Abraham, I had seen some wonderful breakthroughs. Abraham had got his boy at last, the son of promise. Those had been years of trying and hoping as well as doing some creative thinking: Maybe he should have the child through his slave instead of through his wife? After years of heartache, he could enjoy having a son by his side.

We had worked so hard in church planting. We had moved to a different country, given up our pensions, and sold our house. You know, the normal Christian stuff of becoming missionaries without any income, home, or security. We were a family with two small children. It was an adventure and it was scary.

After quite a few years in ministry, we began to see things take off. We had planted several churches in different countries, so our small church movement was gaining ground. Together, we had started projects in our local communities, and we had trained around 180 people on our full-time ministry programme.

We heard about people showing interest in starting some churches in Africa, and there was a vision of starting more churches in India. We had been praying for this opportunity for years and we were seeing things take off. At the same time, it became increasingly difficult to be awarded new contracts to continue our social work in our local community. These contracts were the backbone of our personal income as a family. I was fighting, tendering, and consulting, but things just went from bad to worse.

I came to a standstill. On one hand, God opened doors for ministry, the kind of ministry that we wanted to do, on the other hand, we were losing our financial backing for key ministries and for us as a family. What to do? Abraham was tested and so were we (22:1).

When tested, I often find it challenging to know if it comes from God or the Devil. Discerning spirits is a fine art. I knew I could not just do business as usual and Abraham faced the same challenge.

God asked the impossible of him. He had to take his son to another area, possibly Jerusalem or Samaria ("the land of Moriah"; the exact place is uncertain) and sacrifice him (22:2). It feels so wrong to hear God saying things like that. Can that truly be God's voice? It does not sound like Him, so maybe it is the Devil? I have that kind of internal dialogue whenever God does things in a different way in my life, compared to what I know or have learnt.

We were being blessed with an interest in our church ministry, the kind of multiplication that we had only read about in books. God was coming through, breaking through, but was He? Why did the money not follow the vision? As we would often hear people say, "When God writes the agenda, He underwrites the agenda!" Don't you sometimes get angry with these sound bites and one-liners? I do, but they easily stick in the mind and that makes them powerful. They influence our decision making and affect our discernment. They can easily speak louder than the Bible and the voice of God.

God did not ask me to sacrifice my ministry, but inspired by this story, I felt I had to lay down my ministry while leading a small, international network of churches and projects. It was scary, and people worried about me and my mental state. Abraham was on a three-day trek, but I laid down my ministry during the last four months of 2015. We had ministry opportunities, but no money, which then cancelled out the openings. On top of that, we could not continue what we were already doing, but how could I be the pastor and be the overseer of a church movement if I needed a full-time job outside the movement to feed my family? It would be impossible to go to India, Sri Lanka, or Nepal several times a year to support the churches. I felt stuck. Things looked impossible.

I wonder how Abraham felt, being asked to kill his son (22:2). It was common in society to kill the firstborn son as part of fertility rituals, but that was the other gods demanding that. Would our God do the same? We are not far into the Bible, so there were no holy scriptures, no Jesus, and no Temple priests to ask for advice. Abraham showed what a man of faith would do. He tested the waters. He tested if this was the voice of God or not, and he started walking (22:3).

Abraham did not know exactly where he was going (22:2). He had to walk to the Land of Moriah and find the mountain that God would show him when he got closer. I prefer to know the full road map before I consider taking steps of faith. Just throwing myself into a new venture without a plan does not fit modern management theory! I need to know the WHY, have done the SWOT analysis, considered the work/life balance... Naturally, I need to develop not just a plan A, but also B and C, because a good leader knows that things will go wrong, so I need to be prepared.

Our faith walk is so different when God is speaking to us because it is a matter of learning to trust Him. To trust that God will be there for us, that God will speak to us and that God will be our road map. He will show us which mountain to climb, but we need to move to know the next step. Recently, I have learnt that one of the catch phrases in Ignatian spirituality is, "contemplatives in action." We learn discernment on the move when we look for God in all things.

Taking a four months sabbatical was challenging. I set out not to make any strategic decisions for four months about our ministries. I would not be involved in any teaching, preaching or meetings, but I would keep in contact with my friends and leaders in our churches. My days would be quite scheduled. I would do one hour on the exercise bike, I would listen to TED talks (www.TED.com), I would learn to develop my piano playing skills, and I would seek God.

In the spirit of the text, I would lay down my ministry, in the same way as Abraham was asked to give up his son. He would lose his son, if God did not interfere and likewise, I would give up on my ministry if God did not guide me. One thing is to attempt to do that for ourselves, but we rarely live in a vacuum. Our decisions, even our decisions about ministry, family, vocation, or sabbath affect other people. My sense of responsibility lay heavily on my shoulders. Could I trust God to lead me in a positive way that would also be a blessing to my fellow pastors, leaders, staff, etc.? Believing is tough because there is no guaranteed outcome. I remember that the leader of the Vineyard movement, John Wimber, once said that "faith is spelled R-I-S-K." I can relate to that and that scared me.

There are things that we can share with others, but there are other things that we must do on our own (22:5). Abraham asked the young men to stay behind, as it was time to climb the mountain alone with Isaac. The deadline was moving closer. They had journeyed, but they were close to the end of their journey. I remember the feeling in my stomach and the confusing thoughts in my head. I was moving closer to the end of the four months period and God had been silent. I had received no revelation at all. If God did not come through soon, then my ministry would be over, and I would have to throw the towel in the ring.

I wonder if Abraham acted out of intuition, faith, or conviction? Abraham said to the young men that it was time to worship God, and when they had done that, then Isaac and Abraham would return to them (22:5). Worship?? How can you call it worship when you are going to kill your son? How can you call it worship when you feel that your ministry is going down the drain? But we must worship, because only through following God will we find out if it was the voice of God or not. We need to test the revelation.

The voice of God is rarely found in the spectacular, but through hints from heaven. I would love for God to be in the wind, the earthquake, or the fire, but then following Him would not take faith or discernment. Fellowship does not come through shouting our truths, but from communicating from the depths of our being (1 Kings 19:11-13).

Sure, I would love for God to make things really clear to me. I am open to receiving some great dreams, or people prophesying the same message over me, but when it comes to the big changes in my life, then it has been hints from heaven. I do not know when they come, and they are not impressive, but they are impactful.

Abraham was not a half-hearted man. He went all the way. He had just shared that they would come back after worship, and then he puts his son on the alter (22:9)! What a paradox. Abraham was not used to people coming back from the dead, he had never learnt about Jesus's resurrection or how Jesus raised people from the dead. I do not know what went through his head: Nobody had taught him about making positive confessions! Sarah had not given him "The power of positive thinking" for Christmas or "You can if you think you can" for his birthday.

Deep down Abraham must have known his God and expected God to come through in His own surprising way. Abraham let God be God and he did not try to explain Him or box Him in. He was just obedient to what was asked of him.

How do we answer the people close to us (22:7)? Those who love us and care for us. Those people who are not asking because they are critical, but asking because they see our life, our pain, and our inner turmoil.

Abraham had a fantastic answer. He said that "God will provide for Himself the sheep..." (22:8). God does not need our sacrifices. God does not need for Abraham to kill his son or for me to give up my ministry. God will provide the things that He needs. He is the source of life. What God is looking for is friendship with us, that we listen to His voice and learn to follow His guidance. It is all about fellowship, not rules and regulations, flagellation, or other kinds of self-harm. God does not ask us to kill our dreams or our longings. He does not ask us to give up our children. He is asking us to follow Him, because He is the Way, the Truth, and the Life (John 14:6). And Abraham followed Him to the land of Moriah and found the mountain where God wanted to meet with him. Abraham found God in the quiet on the mountainside.

As Abraham showed his willingness to follow God wherever He might lead him, God put a stop to all the craziness (22:12). Our God is a holy God (a different God), so we do not have to do the stuff that other gods demand of us. There was no reason for Abraham to kill his son, there was no need for me to abandon my calling in life. God does not leave us to ourselves. He gets involved and He is involved as God our Immanuel, the God who is with us.

What was the test all about? It was about faith (22:12). Was Abraham going to recognise and follow the voice of God, or would he dismiss it? We are tested to see if we choose faith or the patterns of the world. "Now I know" is God's answer as He travels with us through life. Like Job, we can worship God, but will we also follow Him when the going gets tough? Nobody knows our response without trials. I cannot even predict all my actions and decision, but God notices our response and He comes to our rescue. God appreciated that Abraham would choose God over his own thinking and feelings. It is expressed with the words "to fear God." I have come to understand that fearing God means to trust God, as the Bible states over 300 times that we shall not fear. Fear may destroy healthy decision making and our physical bodies, but trust and faith make us whole. Abraham did not fear God, as in being scared, but he trusted God's voice and followed Him.

God did respond to Abraham's faith. He did provide a ram for the alter and He did provide a vision for my life.

It was just before the end of my four months sabbatical. It was Christmas time and we were visiting family in Denmark. I went for a walk and as I walked, I sensed that God was renewing His call to me. I understood that He called me to preach, write books and train leaders. When I came back from my walk, I wrote it down in my spiritual journal and told no one. I did ask God to confirm His calling as these three things sounded too good to be true. I would love to spend the rest of my life doing these three things.

On the first Sunday in January 2016 I was preaching in our church in the UK. My sabbatical had come to an end on December the 31st. After the service I was in the kitchen doing the dishes. One of the co-pastors came to me and asked if I had heard the feedback from one of the church members. I said I had heard something, but it would be nice to hear what he had said to him. The co-pastor told me that our church member had said that he felt that I should spend the rest of my life focusing on preaching, writing books and training leaders! My hint from heaven had been confirmed by somebody who knew nothing about my personal revelation. God had provided the answer for me as He did for Abraham. It was not a full answer. I still do not know the how, when, and where but I had been given a new direction in life.

A few months later, everything went pear shaped, but that is another story.

Guilty of a Wasted Life?

Ecclesiastes 2:1-11 (The Message Translation)

2 $^{1-3}$ I said to myself, "Let's go for it - experiment with pleasure, have a good time!" But there was nothing to it, nothing but smoke. What do I think of the fun-filled life? Insane! Inane! My verdict on the pursuit of happiness? Who needs it? With the help of a bottle of wine and all the wisdom I could muster, I tried my level best to penetrate the absurdity of life. I wanted to get a handle on anything useful we mortals might do during the years we spend on this earth.

$^{4-8}$ Oh, I did great things: built houses, planted vineyards, designed gardens and parks and planted a variety of fruit trees in them, made pools of water to irrigate the groves of trees. I bought slaves, male and female, who had children, giving me even more slaves; then I acquired large herds and flocks, larger than any before me in Jerusalem. I piled up silver and gold, loot from kings and kingdoms. I gathered a chorus of singers to entertain me with song, and - most exquisite of all pleasures— voluptuous maidens for my bed.

$^{9-10}$ Oh, how I prospered! I left all my predecessors in Jerusalem far behind, left them behind in the dust. What's more, I kept a clear head through it all. Everything I wanted I took - I never said no to myself. I gave in to every impulse, held back nothing. I sucked the marrow of pleasure out of every task - my reward to myself for a hard day's work!

[11] *Then I took a good look at everything I'd done, looked at all the sweat and hard work. But when I looked, I saw nothing but smoke. Smoke and spitting into the wind. There was nothing to any of it. Nothing.*

ONE OF MY American friends always asked me, "Are we having fun?" It was an interesting question, because in Denmark, we would rather consider if, "we were having a cosy time". Later, as I trained to become a Logotherapist (Dr. Viktor Frankl's psychotherapy), we would ask the question, "Is it meaningful?"

Three different ways to evaluate a situation. Three different world views. Three different answers.

Reading Solomon's writings in Ecclesiastes, I wonder if he missed the mark. Some researchers have suggested that he wrote Song of Songs early in his life, Proverbs in the middle of his life and Ecclesiastes at the end of his life journey. If that is so, then it is depressing reading. You get the impression that life did not work out as he expected. It was all smoke and mirrors. There is a sense of despair as you read through the book.

It is interesting to read such an old passage, and then to consider my own life as a middle-aged, white, educated, middle-class male. I have lived a privileged life in many ways in comparison to many from the lower income countries. I am not sure that I have ever just let lose like Solomon, but I have had the opportunity to have a go at a number of things (2:1-3). My upbringing was influenced by the post-Freudian western culture of pleasure and of having a good time. If it was not harmful to yourself or others, then it was seen as permissible. As I grew up, I was not affected by church morals or the consideration if my actions were honouring God or not. I lived under the sun like Solomon. I made decisions based on my reality, my dreams, and my needs.

As I teenager, this meant drinking, dancing, and just having a laugh. I would test people's reactions in such situations because I could always say that I was drunk, so I did not really mean what I said or did. Also, I tested the waters about being gay. There was no big reaction, but no cathartic moment either. So, I went back into the closet. It was the time when we started hearing about AIDS, so being out and proud was a bit of a challenge to me. My teenage dream was to get involved in politics. I thought it would be great to become the first male MP with a boyfriend/husband (Denmark was the first country to legalise civil partnership in 1989), but I also knew it might be a challenge. I buried that dream too.

Solomon spent his life pursuing happiness and gaining wisdom. It does not sound bad, but it is interesting to notice how he still concluded that it did not lead to a fulfilling life. He did not constrain himself. I cannot but think of the culture we have created in some LGBT+ communities, where we just go for it. No restraints. No filter. After coming out, some of us behave like crazy teenagers no matter our age. It is as if we find it hard to say no to ourselves after all the constraints, we put on ourselves due to our life in the closet. Some of us just want to live life to the full right here and right now. It does not matter if it harms us long-term. We want to live in the now. We let go and we expect others to respect us no matter what we do.

I remember talking to one of the staff at the local supermarket. He was a young gay man. One day he told me proudly how he had been in a police cell after being in a fight with his boyfriend the previous weekend. We may have gained some freedoms, but do we have the freedom to hurt others just because we are LGBT+?

If we let go of any morals and boundaries when seeking excitement, then I wonder if we miss the meaning of life and the purposes of God. In the Book of Romans, we read about God's grace, but freedom does not encourage us to do whatever we feel like. God's way is to encourage us to set boundaries freely. We do not stop ourselves from doing stuff because the church does not like it, but we protect ourselves because we choose to. We do so to honour God who bestows grace on us when we miss the mark.

Solomon tried pleasure and he accomplished things, great things. He set out ambitious plans to plant and build and buy and sell (2:4-8). It did not matter if it was things or people. Everything had become a commodity to him. He bought and sold slaves to his liking. Human trafficking was obviously not an issue for him. He gathered wealth and slept with anybody and everybody. Solomon was making a name for himself, but not for God. People could praise him for the splendour of the buildings, and the many ladies might boost his self-image, but it became a false ego, a false self. Solomon was losing himself like we sometimes lose ourselves in our constant search for looking young and perfect or whatever it takes to attract a hunky guy. Solomon tried to find pleasure and fulfilment in the arms of different women and concluded that all these great opportunities left him empty. We may go from arm to arm, but maybe the deeper desire is for deep sexual and relational intimacy that leads us to the Divine. Our relationships move us closer to or away from God.

When, like Solomon, life is about conquest, the thrill of it all, then keeping up is tough. The constant search, the need for something or somebody better is stressful. I question what some of the apps do to our emotional and spiritual health. Swipe left or swipe right. One was rejected, another was accepted. What does that do to your spirit and your soul, as others also swipe left or right when they see your picture? How many rejections can you cope with every day of every week?

bit heavier? It does not matter if I am in a church ministry or some-where else.

The false spirit will lead me towards endless need for enjoyment, plea-sure seeking and instant gratification. It is about building a name for myself. Solomon lived that life for many years. Only at the end of his life did he notice that it had been an empty life. What could have been inspiring and faith building ended up as an ego trip. Self-actualisation is not necessarily enriching, but the encouragement of the good spirit to serve, to love God and His world will lead to a more purposeful life.

Let us not exchange a meaningful life for an easy life. Let us examine ourselves daily to catch the waves of the Spirit, so that we may be led by God in all things and love God in and through all things. Then we may be enriched by our achievements, our buying and selling, entertainment and deep and meaningful physical and emotional rela-tionships. We can let go of a distorted masculinity where sex is used as a conquest and people are utilised to feed our frail egos. Coming out is not a go free card and a licence to irresponsible behaviour towards others and ourselves. Let us dare to be built up by God's love, grace, and forgiveness, and then to meet the world with hospitality, love, and service. And yes, sex is good, and sex is healthy.

New Territory

Matthew 14:19-36 (David Bentley Hart translation)

19 And, having bidden the crowds to recline upon the grass he took the five loaves and two fishes, looked up to heaven, pronounced a blessing, and broke the loaves and gave them to the disciples, and the disciples to the crowds.

20 And all ate and ate their fill; and they took up what was left over of the fragments, filling twelve baskets.

21 And those eating were about five thousand men, not counting women and children.

22 Then he insisted that the disciples embark into the boat and precede him to the other side, until he should dismiss the crowds.

23 And having dismissed the crowds he ascended the mountain by himself to pray. And when evening arrived he was there alone.

24 But the boat was now many stadia away from land, being tormented by the waves because the wind was adverse.

25 And in the fourth watch of the night he came toward them, walking upon the sea.

26 And the disciples, seeing him walking upon the sea, were disturbed, saying, "It is a phantom," and they cried out in fear.

27 But at once he spoke to them, saying, "Take heart, it is I; do not be afraid."

28 And, answering him, Peter said, "Lord, if it is you, command me to come to you upon the waters."

29 And he said, "Come." And descending from the boat Peter walked on the waters and came toward Jesus.

30 But seeing the blowing wind he was afraid and, beginning to sink, he cried out, saying, "Lord, save me!"

31 And, immediately stretching out a hand, Jesus took hold of him and says, "You of little faith, why did you waver?"

32 And as they went up onto the boat the wind fell.

33 And those in the boat prostrated themselves to him, saying, "Truly you are the Son of God."

34 And, crossing over, they came into the land of Gennesaret.

35 And the men of that place, recognising him, sent out word to the whole region, and brought to him all those who were suffering afflictions,

36 And begged him that they might but touch the fringe of his mantle; and as many as touched it were entirely cured.

(This reflection might be a bit confusing because I have tried to imagine myself as Peter. What would I feel, think, and how might I react? I also bring my personal experiences to the passage to see how the spirit of the passage may help me towards wholeness, integration, and salvation).

IT WAS QUITE a day. We heard the sad news about the murder of John the Baptist just because Herod did not want to lose face. It was a day of sadness and a realisation that doing God's work challenges the power structures of our society. We build kingdoms, businesses, and organisations based on money, power, and prestige, and so we do what we can to keep our power base. Those on the top of the ladder will do many things to stay in power, but at what cost?

How can it be, that a weird looking man like John was a threat to Herod? I am gobsmacked that a simple man like John, who had no army, could stir up so much discontent in the royal court. He spoke truth to power about living a moral life, that was all, but it was enough to release the wrath of the elite.

John was a casualty of war. He tried to make Godly decisions and live a simple life instead of supporting the powerhouses of the region. Is it right that they can get away with anything just because they are rich and powerful?

Personally, I wonder if there are things that I try to get away with that are displeasing to God? What are the decisions I make, the cultural norms I live by and perceive as normal because that is what other people do? Lord, I need you to show me when I miss the mark. I need your Spirit to show me how to take steps closer to you and not away from you. Are there situations where I do something less helpful and honourable, just because I am afraid of feeling like a failure or losing face (14:9)?

Hearing the news was hard on Jesus – well, on all of us. I think Jesus knew this was just one person in a long stream of martyrs throughout the ages. People losing their lives for doing good. Liberation has a price. Jesus knew that. He might have been ok about His own suffering; but seeing the suffering of other people is something else. As He went away to pray (14:13), maybe He thought of the time after His birth when all the boys under the age of two were killed in the area where He was born. It was a slaughter of the innocent. How can anybody see danger in a child? I guess only the paranoid and those caught up in a system where my place in society and in the pecking order is more important than respect for human life. It also shows disrespect for God.

When Jesus returned from prayer, the crowds had gathered (14:14). I wondered how we could show compassion for Him, but instead He showed compassion for others. He healed and prayed and prayed and healed all day long (14:15). There was no time for TLC (Tender, Loving, Care) or selfcare for Jesus. Instead, He poured out his life and gave to others what He needed Himself. I was deeply impressed. I wanted to send the crowds away. Let's have a day to grieve and to talk things through. The situation also affected our lives. Would we be safe ministering alongside Jesus? Some of us had families to look after. We were used to all the verbal battles, but murder! Naturally, we were used to the Roman war machine, but they usually focused on rebels using violence to try to overthrow the Roman government or at least the Roman occupation.

Jesus was different. I am getting used to that, but it surprised me anyway. After praying for the sick all day, He focused on their hunger. He was not just going the second mile while being distraught himself, he was so eager to show another way. The way of love. A practical love that permeates body and soul.

I am not sure what I saw right in front of my eyes. I saw the crowds, I saw an impossible situation, I saw food that can only feed a handful of people and yet, Jesus trusted that God would do something unique. Then Jesus asked us to feed people, turning five loaves of bread and two fish into a proper meal for thousands of people (14:19).

I have often faced impossible situations, and during such times I find it hard to notice anything but the challenges. Even when I have had a breakthrough and want to tell others about it, I so easily fall into the trap of focusing more on the things that still need to be solved.

My mind is bent towards the challenges, but not so with Jesus. God is in some way wrapped up in His whole being. He does not compartmentalise His life. He does not have a spiritual life, a working life, a family life, etc. Jesus is a truly integrated person and He trusts God for all aspects of His life. I need to get hold of that. He is showing me that faith is not just for the professional people at the Temple or the religious leaders in the synagogues. Spirituality permeates everything. This pushes my understanding of the spiritual and the secular. Jesus lives in an integrated way. How attractive that is. He makes God relevant to me, He is an authority in making faith work.

You should have seen their faces when they could just keep on eating (14:20). Some people had not had a lot to eat for days and some had only had some bread. Eating fish and as much as you like, was a true celebration. Some people were bursting with joy. They had been healed from awful diseases and now they could even enjoy a great meal too. We were all learning a lesson about feasting on God and what it will be like in the Kingdom of God. The laughter, the chatter, and the prayers of thanks still fill my mind. It was a life changing experience.

As people were finishing their meal, Jesus came to us and asked us to get going (14:22). He wanted us to get a head start on our journey to the next town. It had already been a long day and we were exhausted.

I was in two minds. What about Jesus Himself? He was grieving, He had healed people all day, and He had fed the multitudes. What about His needs? I guess He needed time alone (14:23). It was His way of dealing with things. He needed to pray. To find peace to sustain Him. To make sense of His feelings and thoughts in the presence of God. He needed a God moment to deal with the matters of the day. He would be ok; I could relax and get on with our travel arrangements together with the others.

We were tired. Well, that is not the whole truth. We were exhausted. I was happy that Jesus sent us off, so we could get going, but we were going to travel all night. One thing is to travel all night after a long day at work, it is something else when the wind suddenly goes from bad to worse (14:24). It was just awful. None of us could sleep, only hope for the best. Would we be able to survive this crazy storm that was tormenting our boat and our emotional state? I am no fisherman, so I was not keen on this kind of weather, to say it the least, but seeing my friends being scared did not exactly give me great confidence. We had four experienced fishermen in our band of brothers, and they fought against the wind with all their might. We did all the right things, but the elements were tearing our lives apart. I was reminded of some of those battles in ministry, where people are attacking us from all sides. No matter what we do, they have something to criticise. There have been times in ministry when it was just all too much.

I am reminded of a time that sucked life out of me. It was summertime and God spoke to me about a new season in ministry. We would experience a time where things would become easier and more people would respond to our work. I was thrilled.

A few weeks later, things went bad. My daughters were about nine and eleven and they got the flu and so did my ex. Well, there is nothing special about a flu except it did not burn out within some days or even weeks. My ex was ill for about three months, my oldest daughter for about six months. After a recovery period, she got ill again. My youngest was ill for a year. She could not go to school, she got depressed and cried for hours every day. Her personality changed, and I could not recognise her. Come Easter, she also lost her ability to walk. We tried everything. We saw a specialist several times, she was offered teaching at home from the local authorities, but she was too ill to cope even with just five minutes of teaching. She also received physiotherapy treatments, but nothing helped.

It was an evil year. I had to keep the church together, the social work and my family. Even when my ex returned to work in the ministry, we experienced criticism at work and illness at home. What to do, where to turn? God felt so far away. He was not in the boat of our lives. He seemed far away, and I was torn on the inside watching my family suffer because of a stupid flu virus that got stuck in their bodies somehow. Where was God in all of this? Where were the blessings in ministry that He had told me about? Instead, it felt like everything was being destroyed from the inside out. As with the brothers in the boat, we were all tired and did not know the next step that would take us out of that destructive crushing wind of life. We felt like Satan was having the upper hand and it was not good.

Early in the morning, at some point between 3 and 6am, Jesus decided to catch up with us (14:25). We did not get it as He was walking on the water. That was not His usual way, so naturally we got scared (14:26). Was this healthy Christian spirituality or was this deep deception? When you are scared, tired, and desperate you can easily get it wrong. And we were desperate for help.

One of the things that I admire about Jesus, is His incredibly creative ways. He kept us on our toes, but it was difficult to discern what was going on and whether this was bad theology, bad spirituality, or a distorted view of God, or even worse: the inspiration of the anti-Christ? Have you ever faced that dilemma? You are desperate for some answers and you will do almost anything. The scheme promising quick results, suddenly sounds like God's answer to your prayers. Any treatment must be God's way of dealing with your ailments. Any business deal or job opportunity looks attractive.

When under pressure, I find it difficult to discern what is the right thing to do. How do I protect myself and others from unhelpful solutions, and at the same time stay open to God's surprises and Divine appointments? It is challenging having a tough mind and a soft heart. Balancing the two, demands real wisdom from God.

We got it so wrong as we struggled to survive in that boat. We thought it was a ghost since Jesus had never walked on water before. It was not a pretty sight having a boat full of grown-up men seasoned by hard labour scream in fear. We could not constrain ourselves. We were drained of all life and energy. We could not cope with yet another thing to deal with.

Then Jesus came close to us. He told us that it was Him and there was nothing to fear (14:27). How often we need to hear that, and I need to hear that. Worry is a frequent, unwelcome guest in my life.

I am astonished how difficult it is for me to trust God and let His love melt away my fearful thoughts and emotions. It is obviously a big deal for me to trust God and others. Maybe it is due to the many years of hiding, the fear of HIV, the panic about being found out, and all the voices of homophobia that I have listened to. I would like to take baby steps towards trusting God again. I could do with little bits of faith to transform my soul and my thinking.

Maybe that was the reason for my stupid request? I also wanted to be able to function in a new environment (14:28). In coming out, I knew that the rules would change from one moment to another, but I did not have the experience or the knowledge of how to deal with it and what to expect. I was entering a new dimension very much on my own.

Jesus welcomed me out of the boat (14:29). Being in that boat with the tormenting wind was not easy. All those years of pushing down all thoughts of me being gay was not exactly a walk in the park. All the different voices and emotions were not a healthy place to stay. It had been a bumpy ride for all too long. It would be nice to get out of that boat.

I was not in two minds when Jesus said, "Come." I was out of that boat faster than you can say any homophobic swearwords to my face. My time had come, and it was a time with Jesus. It was not a time walking away from Jesus, quite the opposite. I know that it does not fit with the views of some Christian pastors and commentators, but I walked straight towards Jesus.

It was time for the liberation that I had been praying for. I had to leave the crowd behind, their expectations and wishes. I had to stand on my own two feet trusting that Jesus would walk the walk with me. And – there was no turning back. I would never want to conform and pretend again. No more straight acting. When you take a step of faith it changes you. It gives you a deep sense of fear as well as satisfaction, and those choices shape you and your future.

I wish I could say that life became plain sailing after that. The surprises and the opposition became too hard to handle. I cried out to Jesus as I have done so many times before (14:30). I needed His salvation from the oppression of the church; the lies, the misuse of power, the loss of ministry. It was such a humiliating experience being stripped from your dignity and identity. It meant the world to me to be Rev, Dr. Arno Steen Andreasen.

How gracious our Jesus is! He rescued me, not because I was right, deserved it, or because I am a saint (14:31). He liberated me and protected me because I am loved. I do not need to live up to the expectations of the church or society. I do not need to worry about the power struggles within the church hierarchy. I need to follow Jesus and I am grateful for His saving grace. He pulled me up, gave me a new start.

As Jesus saved me, He also lifted an eyebrow. He asked me why I had lost faith in Him? Lost faith in the process? Did I really believe that things would just work out without any problems? Why did I not trust Him for the support needed for the journey? Surfing the waves of life and of His Holy Spirit takes both skill and experience, but also trust in Him who upholds us. I lost Jesus for a moment in all the confusion. I became despondent. Suddenly, I was back in Denmark after 18 years in the UK. I had tried to get a job in the UK without luck and I was also trying in Denmark. I had no positive responses for ten months. I did not know what to do or where to turn. I walked up and down the streets of Copenhagen for hours each day. I prayed; *"I lift up my eyes to the hills. From where does my help come? My help comes from the Lord, who made heaven and earth"* (Psalm 121:1-2, ESV). Then at last, the answer came through: I was invited for a job interview and a few weeks later I also had my own place to live. The blessings started to flow, and God showed me that He was still the God of miracles.

It is a unique experience when things start to fall into place. When all the solutions have been aligned, and the pieces are coming together. The tormenting wind had been silenced at last. There is peace within and without. The disturbing voices have lost their power over me at least for a time.

It was the same with my daughter's illness. One day, after almost a year, we were sitting outside in the garden. She could not walk, she had been out of school for a year and it was the summer holiday. She was sitting on the trampoline in the garden with a friend from school. I went on the trampoline and jumped a bit while they sat down. It was good to giggle again after all the pain and suffering of the last year. There was no healing in sight. Suddenly she said to us: "I think I can walk!" She jumped down from the trampoline and started to walk. Then she went outside the house and ran up and down the street. She had not walked for months. It was wonderful. Our daughter was released from her illness. The day after, she went on a holiday to Wales and after the summer holiday she was back in school. Jesus had made our lives liveable again. He had calmed the storms of illness and delivered her from pain.

It is in these moments that we get a new and fresh revelation of Jesus (14:33). I saw that the teachings of Jesus are not just good for comfort, but the words of Jesus are a living reality. Jesus transforms lives today and makes us whole. Jesus takes us out of our boat, out of our hiddenness among other people, and makes us individuals. He liberates us from the tormenting voices and abusive behaviours. He is our safe harbour. Gay or straight, we can depend on Him. He is not a God of the few, but a God of the many. We can turn to Him for a healing touch as well as for the ability to walk in faith as LGBT+ Christians in what may sometimes be a hostile (church) world (14:36).

A Vision for A Better Tomorrow

Acts 10:1-20, 34-35, 44-48 (David Bentley Hart Translation)

*1 Now a certain man in Caesarea by the name of Cornelius –
a centurion from a military cohort called the Italic,*

*2 A devout man and one who along with all his household
revered God, donating many alms to the people and always
supplicating God –*

*3 Clearly saw in a vision, around about the ninth hour of the
day, an angel of God coming in to him and saying to him,
"Cornelius."*

*4 And, gazing at him and growing terrified, he said, "What
is it, lord?" And he said to him, "Your prayers and your
almsgiving have risen up as a memorial offering before God.*

*5 And now send men to Joppa and summon back a certain
Simon, who is also called Peter;*

*6 This man is lodged with a certain Simon, a tanner whose
household is by the sea."*

*7 And as the angel who was speaking to him departed, he
called two of the household slaves and a devout soldier from
among those in constant attendance on him,*

8 And, explaining everything to them, sent them to Joppa.

*9 And the next day, as they were journeying and approach-
ing the city, Peter ascended around the sixth hour up to the
roof to pray.*

10 And he became hungry, and wished to taste some food; and as they were preparing it an extasy came upon him,

11 And he beholds the sky opened, and an object descending, like a great sheet being let down to the ground by four corners,

12 On which were all the quadrupeds and reptiles of the earth and birds of the sky.

13 And a voice came to him: "Arise, Peter, sacrifice and eat."

14 But Peter said, "Certainly not, Lord, for I have never eaten anything profane and impure."

15 And again, for a second time, there came a voice to him: "Do not deem profane what God has made pure."

16 And this happened three times, and at once the object was taken up into the sky.

17 And, as Peter was wondering within himself what the vision he had seen might be, look: The men who had been sent by Cornelius, inquiring after the household of Simon, were standing at the gate,

18 And calling out they asked, "Is Simon, also called Peter, perhaps lodged here?"

19 And as Peter was pondering the vision the Spirit said, "See, two men are seeking you;

20 But rise and go down, and go with them, hesitating over nothing, for I have sent them."

34 And, opening his mouth, Peter said, "In truth, I perceive that God is not a respecter of persons;

35 Rather, in every people, whoever reveres him and performs works of righteousness is accepted by him;

44 While Peter was still uttering these words, the Spirit, the Holy One, feel upon all those listening to the discourse,

45 And the faithful among the circumcised, as many as had accompanied Peter, were astonished, because the gift of the Holy Spirit has been poured out even upon the gentiles;

46 For they heard them speaking in tongues and praising God's greatness. Then Peter spoke up:

47 "Can anyone forbid the water for baptising these persons, who have also received the Spirit, the Holy One, just as we did?"

48 And he instructed them to be baptised in the name of Jesus the Anointed. Then they asked him to remain for a few days.

OUR IDENTITY IS made up of different aspects of our lives. All our experiences, genetics, choices, and God-given uniqueness are knitted together. It is no wonder that we have endless discussions about nature versus nurture when discussing the actions of the individual. Then add SOGI (Sexual Orientation and Gender Identities) to the mix, and we are guaranteed to have a disagreement. Everybody has a stake in it, because the answer affects inclusion versus discrimination, boundaries for behaviour, as well as who is in and who is out.

Did we choose to become a sexual minority or were we assigned a sexual orientation and a gender identity from birth? Do the LGBT+ communities consist of two, five or ten percent of the population? I wonder if it really makes a difference in the end. Isn't it more compassionate to include people and to value others whether they belong to a sizable group in society or not? The Kingdom of God is not about power through size, money, or status. The Jesus way is about bringing God's loving grace to anybody and everybody.

Cornelius was an outsider. He was a minority person on several parameters. He was a Gentile, which meant he was not a Jew, he was a soldier of high rank in the hierarchy of the Roman war machine, as well as a God-believer (10:1-2). He did not fit into the Roman culture, nor did he fit into the Jewish community where he represented the oppressors.

We do not know if he experienced minority stress, as we may do in the LGBT+ communities, because of his power and influence due to his position in society, but it could still leave him lonely and isolated.

No matter what; he was a man of God. One of those surprising people who suddenly show up, and who do not fit the mould of our faith communities. What to do with such people, and can we trust them? They look like people of faith, but are they deceived, and are we being deceived by them? I can see it with my brothers and sisters in the faith. I have heard it said that a gay man like me cannot be a true Christian and that I am a false prophet. I am heading for hell no matter what I proclaim, what I believe, and what I do. I am told that I am an abomination to God.

Years ago, it was popular for speakers to say that we from the LGBT+ communities were idol worshippers, no matter our faith and our beliefs. What, then, are people to think when we come out to them? How can they see us for who we really are? From tradition they know what to conclude, in the same way as Peter knew what to think about Gentiles like Cornelius. They were not God's people, they were not included in God's Kingdom, and they were not predestined to be saved. They were so spiritually unclean that he would not even speak to a person like Cornelius, and he would in no way enter his house. Cornelius was unclean not because of what he did or did not do, but for being. Being alive was enough to make him unclean. He would never be good enough as a person of faith. He had to choose to obey all the 613 laws in the Old Testament and he had to get his foreskin cut off. Then and only then might he stand a chance. Does that sound familiar to us in the LGBT+ communities?

We read about two visions from God. Some might have an issue with the message. Could it really be from God and would God speak to an unclean person in the same way as to a Jew? We notice that God speaks to all His children created in His image, including a Gentile and an outsider, because Cornelius was not an outsider to God.

Cornelius recognised God's voice immediately (10:3-6). He was asked to go and meet Peter. He did not have any issue with that. God had spoken and there was no reason to question the wisdom in that. He had not been conditioned as to what to believe about the way God speaks and what He might say. Cornelius listened with an open mind and God heard his prayers and noticed his generosity (10:4). Cornelius had a private faith and a public faith. He had a belief, but it was a faith in action. May we learn to recognise the Spirit at work in people's lives, so we do not overlook the unlikely saints among us.

Personally, I write a spiritual journal, sometimes daily, at other times several times a week. I write about matters of my heart. I write specific prayers, but I also ask God to inspire me. Then I sit at the keyboard writing whatever I think God might be saying to me. I do that uncritically, so as not to stop the flow of the writing. Afterwards I try to discern if it was from God or just my own imagination. This prophetic exercise has helped me to move closer to the heart of God, to listen and not just to talk, and to earth and mirror my life in Scripture and revelation.

Peter went to a quiet place to pray (10:9). He was hungry, and we see that God used an illustration about food to get Peter's attention (10:10). Maybe that is one of the reasons why Peter questioned the vision (10:14). Could it really be God speaking to him or was it just his desperate need for a meal?

Peter could not accept what God told him. He had been taught that certain foods (and people) were unclean, but now God declared them clean. It had to be a misunderstanding. The Old Testament laws were clearly laid out. There was nothing to debate, and yet God put aside those laws. Peter knew his fellow apostles would be upset. They would follow the ancient prescriptions of how to live holy lives. They knew what not to do, and yet God was telling him to disregard Old Testament rules. Peter had a high view of Scripture, but he had to do away with his classic interpretation of Scripture. It must have been a shock to him.

Because of Peter's training in the faith, he knew it could not be true. He refused to accept what God was saying to him. God had to speak to him three times before it sunk in (10:16). God was serious. The rules had to change. The Gentiles were to be accepted into the Kingdom of God. God is a missionary God and therefore an inclusive and affirming God.

That was my own experience when God spoke to me years ago. He said, "I am not going to heal you, because you are not broken. You have been faithful to your family and the church." I was relieved and I was shocked. It was the best news I had ever heard from God, but how could I be sure it was from God? I returned to the Scriptures to search for answers. I also bought a lot of books on the Bible, relationships, and same-sex marriage. I read different views, I reread Christian counselling books from my early years as a Christian. I came to understand, 34 years after I became a Christian, that there were other ways to interpret Scripture than what I had learnt. I had got stuck in a tradition that was harmful to me, but I did not know any better. I tried to be a good Christian even when I felt something did not add up. It was not until I had this revelation from God that I went back to study the Scriptures with an open heart and mind, researching what a variety of pastors and scholars said about the subject. This revelation and my additional studies offered me great freedom and a stronger conviction of God's all-inclusive love, so I concluded that it was God speaking to me.

There is a place for me in God's Kingdom, even as an out gay man longing for a life-long relationship with another man. I have learnt that the Bible does not say anything about a stable, life-long relationship between two of the same sex, but it does say that it is not good for people to be alone. I am hopeful that one day, I will get the chance to say "I do" in front of God with my husband by my side knowing that I will not be excommunicated from the Kingdom of God.

The visions of Cornelius and Peter totally changed world mission. The Christian faith was not just for the Jews, but Peter belonged to a faith with worldwide implications. No more racism within the Christian faith. It was time to invite the whole world to join the banquet.

Jesus loved to reinterpret Scripture to help people get a truer picture of God. He said things like, *"you have heard that it was said.... But I say to you"* (Matthew 5:21-22) Sometimes we do not get God, and so He speaks into our lives about changing our position. It was no problem for Cornelius who belonged to the minority, but it was a huge issue for Peter, the privileged one from the majority grouping.

Peter knew gentiles had to become fully Jewish to be included in the faith, but now God told him that it was about circumcision of the heart. Salvation is based on who we love and who we follow: No more rituals, no more pretending, no more conformity. Faith is a matter of the heart and of following Jesus.

We see how the revelations to two different people representing two different people groups changed our classic interpretation of Scripture. Because of that, we have a new theology emphasising the inclusiveness of God for the last 2,000 years.

When Cornelius arrived, Peter had come to his senses. He had accepted that God did not divide people into male and female, slave or free, Jew or Gentile. God does not categorise people the way we do (10:34). Peter had come to realise that salvation and inclusion into the Kingdom of God has nothing to do with foreskin or laws. Rather, God is looking for people who honour Him and do justice (10:35). Notice that in line with this revelation, the Holy Spirit was released when Peter spoke (10:44). His ministry was changed, but so was his preaching. People were being blessed in new ways. This convinced other believers that Peter had got the revelation and new interpretation right (10:45). The Gentiles spoke in tongues and praised God because of the new flow of God's Spirit (10:45-46).

The Christians did not conclude that the Gentiles were deceived, or that a false spirit was influencing them. Instead, they recognised God's hand upon the outsiders. As a result, Peter went even further. Nobody should be able to question the validity of their faith and their salvation. Therefore, he baptised them into the mystical Body of Christ (10:47-48). We cannot see the whole Body of Christ, but we see people of faith. This baptism sealed the revelations and the experience.

Maybe what we need is more revelation from God to change the debate and the practices of the church at large. I am not sure that many panel discussions will lead us to unity in regard to LGBT+ Christians, but it looks to me as if revelation and the sealing of the Holy Spirit can make a huge difference – at least it did in the early church. This is how true renewal looks like.

It is my prayer, that God will pour out His revelation upon us all, and that God will confirm His calling and salvation of believers within the LGBT+ communities. May the Body of Christ see that LGBT+ Christians pray and work for justice just like Cornelius, so that they may also welcome us. May the church, in all her diversity, be united.

May God speak to us and empower us to make a difference in this world. May God heal our broken hearts and broken relationships, so that we may be a light on a hill for people to find their way home to God.

May God empower us to heal, save, and deliver people from all evil done in His name. May your Kingdom come, your will be done on earth as it is in heaven.

Stand Up Straight

John 5:1-16 (David Bentley Hart Translation)

1 After these things there was a festival of the Judeans, and Jesus went up to Jerusalem

2 Now at the sheep's gate in Jerusalem there is a pool. Which in Hebrew is called Bethesda, having five porches.

3 A great many of the ill lay in them – the blind, the lame, the withered – (waiting for the movement of the waters.

4 For an angel descended into the pool at a certain time and bestirred the waters; whoever then, after the stirring of the waters stepped in first was healed of whatever disease he had).

5 And there was a certain man there who had had an ailment for thirty-eight years;

6 Jesus, seeing this man lying there and knowing he had already done so for a long time, says to him, "Do you wish to become healthy?"

7 The sick man answered him, "Lord, I have no man who might place me in the pool when the water is stirred; rather, as I approach someone else goes down ahead of me."

8 Jesus says to him, "Arise, take your pallet and walk."

9 And immediately the man became well, and took his pallet and walked. And it was on a Sabbath.

10 So the Judaeans said to the man who had been healed, "It is a Sabbath, and it is not lawful for you to carry the pallet."

11 But he answered them, "The one making me well, that one told me, "Take your pallet and walk.""

12 They asked him, "Who is the man telling you, "Take and walk"?"

13 But the man who had been healed had no idea who it was; for, there being a crowd in that place, Jesus had withdrawn.

14 Afterward Jesus finds him in the Temple and said to him, "See, you have become well: sin no more, so that something worse may not happen to you.

15 The man went away and told the Judeans that Jesus is the one who had made him well.

16 And so the Judaeans persecuted Jesus for having done these things on a Sabbath day.

(This reflection might be a bit confusing, because I have tried to imagine myself as the certain man. What would I feel, think, and how might I react? I also integrate my personal story to see how the spirit of the passage may help me towards wholeness, integration, and salvation).

IT WAS A normal day around the pool (5:3). We were all lying there as usual. It was such a weird situation, but we had gotten used to it. We were gravely ill. If not, we would be out begging or working, but for us, this lot, we could only hope for the best.

The pool was a place of despair. There was so much hopelessness and pain. It was worse than a hospital because we all crowded around one pool. It was an asylum of the outcasts, the people at the margins of society. We were a funny bunch. We came from all walks of life, but we had one thing in common; we were diseased, dysfunctional, and distressed. It was not a nice place to be. Too much hopelessness, too much despair, but there was also a funny kind of kinship. We were all in the same boat, and society preferred it to stay that way. Out of sight, out of mind. We were stigmatised because we were ill, and people believed that God had judged us and left us behind. I think I believed that too some of the time. Lying there among the crowds of desperate people could be very lonely.

The competition was a hard pill to swallow (5:4). There was only one lucky one whenever the angel showed up. We never knew when that would happen. Will it be today or tomorrow or in a week from now? We just had to be there all the time in case the angel made an appearance.

There was a hard lesson to learn from lying around the pool. The winner takes it all. Only one person, the lucky one, would get healed. Can you imagine, only one person out of this crowd of people? That person had to be quick, and the person had to be quite able bodied to get into the pool before anybody else. But what about me? I cannot move, so will I ever by able to get in first? I have tried and tried, believe me.

The pool offered hope, but also discouragement. You should hear the sounds and see the faces when we noticed any movement of the waters. We knew that if we could just get into that water, then the miracle would happen. The whole place changed the moment the angel showed up. There was so much faith and hope, but it all came crashing down within a microsecond. It just took the first person to get into the water and then everybody else knew that it was not their lucky day.

It is easy to question God when that happens. Does He play favourites? Are the physically able closer to God's heart because the rules are made in their favour.

It is like a Divine lottery, but the game is unfair. Some stand a better chance to receive their miracle than others. How is this different from the ways of the world? It is built on injustice and it looks like God is doing the same thing, but I cannot give up. I will not give up. For me just showing up is a sign of hope even if the flame of hope is not burning that brightly.

It is hard playing by somebody else's rules. Unfair rules. What have I done to deserve this?

Do you know how long I have prayed for God to change me? 38 years (in the passage, 34 years for me personally)! Can you imagine what it takes to pray, to hope, to try every rule in the book, to listen to people's advice, and it has not made any difference at all. 34/38 years! If you knew what I have been through during this time. The prayers, the fasting, the deliverance. I have tried to pray the gay away, quoted Scriptures, proclaimed my new identity in Christ, put on the mask to fit in and look like a good straight man. Fake it till you make it, as they said. Decades in the closet, decades in hiding. I have done everything in my power to conform to the straight world, but it has left me crippled. I have lived a double-life and see where it has led me. I am in a bigger mess today than I was before. I hide away around the pool, at the margins of society. I am accepted if I do not stand out: Do not be too flamboyant, do not become a crusader, how can you expect to be respected if you parade your sexuality! I have heard it all and it is crushing me, destroying my sense of self. But I am still here. I cannot afford to give up. I believe but help my unbelief. I know by the end of the day I am still the one with the ailment. I am still living in hiding, alone among the crowd.

Did I get it right? Did that man really see me (5:6)? Can you imagine how I felt? I am no longer just a man in the crowd. I am an individual. I am spotted, I am noticed. This is so different. Right now, I have experienced the feeling of not being overlooked, not being rejected. A stranger looks at me and speaks to me. At first, I cannot believe my luck. As he moves closer to me, I get the impression that he cares for me. He has room in his heart for somebody like me. This is a new experience and I am bursting on the inside. I am not sure how to handle it. A stranger takes an initiative to get to know me. Doesn't he know that the religious people believe that it is my own fault. Somebody must have sinned for me to be in this position. Maybe my parents, maybe me, but somebody is to blame for this condition. It doesn't look like it bothers him!

I must admit, I was confused when he asked me: *"Do you wish to become healthy?"* I did not expect such a question. This was the Bethesda Pool. The pool of healing. Why does he think that I am lying here? I was not on a picnic or here for a casual visit. I wondered if he was poking fun at me. The purpose for me being here, right here, was no surprise to anyone. We were all here for the same reason. We were desperate to receive our miracle and be able to live, really live. We wanted to be with our families again without them being ashamed of us.

I wanted to tell him that I have wasted decades of my life lying here. It has been so frustrating. There have been so many false starts. Times when I thought I was becoming normal, so I could be integrated back into society.

Maybe he does not know how this works, so I tried to explain it to him (5:7). Instead of saying, "yes of course I want to get healed, that is why I have been lying here for 34/38 years," I told him my predicament: I simply cannot get into the pool quick enough. Something happened within me as I told him how it works. I felt the stirring of the Spirit. Maybe he is my saviour, my helper, my midwife who is going to help me be born again as I get baptised into the waters and become one with my God. I know it takes a new birth, a new beginning to get healed, untangled from the words spoken over me and their crippling effect on my body, soul, and spirit.

I have tried, really tried to do my best, but my best has never been good enough. Do you know what that does to your self-image and self-acceptance? How can I accept and love myself when God does not seem to bother with me? Something deeply disturbing must be wrong with me. Maybe all the different people, religious people, are right: I am just a pervert, doomed to hell, an idol worshipper. If I truly loved God, then I would not be like this. I would be able to straighten up and walk with my head held high.

Things went from weird to bizarre. The stranger told me to stand up (5:8). This was the exact thing that I could not do. His words were easy to understand, but maybe that was why they sounded so strange to my ears. I had to stand up and walk away with my mat. It was as if he was telling me that I was not going to spend more time around the pool, but I needed the pool to heal me. I needed the angel to arrive. I needed somebody to help me into the pool. That was the rule, didn't he get it? That was what I have been told all these years. I had to follow the rules, wanting the healing badly enough and then my healing would come.

My mind worked overtime. All thinking, all logic, all arguments, and everything that I have learnt and believed was challenged. I had this inner fight because I knew the religious teaching.

The thing is, he spoke with clarity. He spoke with authority. He spoke to me like nobody else. Only one thing was required of me and he said, "stand up."

What did I have to lose? Naturally, I would be humiliated and become the laughingstock of the pool community, when I tried and failed, but he looked at me. He noticed me. There was a connection and I was not alone anymore in my struggles. I felt that he was with me, so why ignore him. Why ignore his advice even though it went against the principles of healing!

I had prayed so many times. Could he be the answer?

So many thoughts went through my mind in a split second. Should I respond to the confusion or to his voice? It was a voice of hope so I had no choice. I had to respond, I had to try. Maybe this was my time.

In the blinking of an eye it happened to me (5:9). I received my healing. I could walk again. I was a changed man. It happened so suddenly and a whole new reality took over. It was surreal. I felt like a human being. Now, I could accept myself. All this evil was over. The night had become day. It was a new season. I was at home in my body for the first time. I was whole.

I was liberated on a Sabbath. Sabbath never really meant anything to me. It was a day like any other day. I was ill. I needed healing. I was lying by the pool. Sabbath was a nice idea for the others who were fully welcomed in the synagogues and the Temple, but it was no place for me. I was the crippled one, so I was not welcome in the house of God. Normal people could take steps closer to God and normal, that was not me.

Today, I understand what Sabbath is about. My healing and my liberation, that was my Sabbath. A day like no other day. A day lived for God. A day to seek His Kingdom and His righteousness and everything else will be given to you. But it was the stranger taking the initiative. It was not me. I was just available by the pool. He came over, he noticed me, he spoke to me. I responded, that was all. I responded to his call. I followed his lead.

Now, I know that I was created for the Sabbath. I was not created for luck, illness, body-shaming, or self-hatred. I was created for God.

Nothing happened as expected, but it happened fast. My healing came immediately. He spoke, I stood up and my life will never be the same again.

But – there are Sabbath traditions and people were quick to remind me of them (5:10). I had received my miracle and now they began to attack me, you know, the faith people. They told me that I could not carry my mat! Should I care about religious statues right now? I was healed, my life had been transformed. How come that they are not happy for me? I am no longer twisted in body, soul, and spirit.

What are these rules about anyway? I thought I was going to get healed by getting into the water, but not so. I thought I was supposed to take my mat home with me as I did not need my spot anymore. This was confusing, but I also felt a bit angry. I got my life back or maybe it is truer to say: Now, I have a life!

Why did they want to know who asked me to take my mat home with me (5:11-13)? Isn't that irrelevant? Let's focus on the main thing. I was lost, but now I am found. I was dying of shame, self-doubt, and self-hatred, but now I live in freedom. First things first guys, but they kept going. I am not sure I can really cope with this interrogation. I have been here for 34/38 years and they never showed me any attention. They never helped me or supported me and now they question me because things are not happening the way their religious traditions prescribe.

How do I respond to Christian leaders in the right way? They push me away from fellowship when I do not conform to their traditions and Bible interpretations and they question my faith when I do well.

I have picked up my mat in good faith. Why should I not follow the lead of the man who made me well?

I was not sure about his name. He did not tell me, but I followed his lead. Isn't that the right thing to do, to listen and respond to the one who liberated me, who offered me a lifeline, who noticed me when others had written me off.

I am beginning to think that it is important who you listen to. Some voices set you free while others crush your happiness and question your faith and integrity. I refuse to be intimidated. The stranger told me to stand and I will stand up for him and he asked me to follow his lead. He stood by me and I will stand by him. He cared for me, while they cared about their laws and they did not heal me. The religious teaching condemned me to 34/38 years as a slave to their expectations. All I know is that now I live in freedom and I follow the stranger's advice. My life was transformed and that feels good. I am on my way and I will not allow anybody to take that away from me again. I am stronger now, more at ease with myself. I am me.

I considered what to do with my new life and decided that there is only one right thing to do. I wanted to worship at the Temple (5:14). I had not been to the Temple as I was not welcome. Now I can go and thank God for my life. I can go and tell Him how much I love Him. My decision to follow the stranger's lead has helped me to take steps closer to God. Can you imagine, I can be part of a worshipping community. I want to be in His courts. I want to sing His praises.

At the Temple I meet the stranger again. Again, he took the initiative to talk to me. His name was Jesus. What a good name. It suits Him as He did become my Saviour. I can easily call Him that. It feels good.

Jesus told me to "see", to notice that God is good. He is rewriting my understanding of God. Instead of the God of luck, the God who played favourites, I see a God who is making everything new. I am learning to notice the work of God.

He told me not to fall into sin again. I need to walk in faith. I need to make a commitment not to embrace a toxic faith again, a faith that destroyed my relationship with God, a faith that took away my true identity. I will no longer wear a mask; I will no longer live a double life. I will no longer hide. I am gay and I am created in God's image. When I try to conform to a straight-acting lifestyle, then I am dishonest. I am rejecting who I am, and I am rejecting God and His purpose for my life.

I need to embrace my wild card. Yes, I am different, but that does not mean I am wrong. That does not mean that I am not patterned after God. Rejecting myself and focusing on other people's expectations will destroy my life, my ministry, and my relationship with God.

I asked God to forgive me for trying to live and pretend to be straight. I asked the Creator God for forgiveness for devaluing my uniqueness and my purpose in life. I was created for a purpose; I was created by a loving God. I am not an emotional cripple, I am not a pervert, I am not emotionally immature just because I am attracted to other men. I am a lover and I am the beloved.

Trying to be somebody that I am not is a sin. That is play acting. That is being a hypocrite. I laid down my old life at the altar and Jesus picked me up. I was in a real state. Now I need to learn to live life as a follower of Jesus, my Saviour. No longer shall I live a life of shame, guilt, and condemnation. No longer shall I feel crippled or look down upon by myself because I believed God looked down upon me. For a long time, I thought that God was disappointed in me.

Jesus told me to lay aside all these things. It is time to live authentically. It is time to let my light shine. The whole me. Only then, can

God really use me. His power can flow through me when I am transparent, honest, and authentic.

My weakness was not being gay. My sin was my lack of confidence in God. The God who created me for good works. The God who created me to love Him and His people. I can love me because He loved me first. I am His beloved and He knows my name.

I cannot go back. I have closed a door to my past life trying to conform to the expectations of the culture, the church, and the people around me. Jesus broke through all the religious rules and He touched me by His Spirit. I want to honour Him, the God of surprises. I will walk in faith.

I can answer them now (5:15-16). I know His name and His name is Jesus. They can look at my life. They can evaluate the fruit of my life. I am part of a church fellowship, but for some reason, that is not enough for some.

They are not happy for me. They questioned me and when they finished questioning me, then they had a go at Jesus. Why do some people want to put up barriers for others who experience the liberating love of God? Why are they not happy for me and my new freedom? My life was transformed in the blinking of an eye. I thought that I would become straight through all the prayers, the deliverance, the fasting, the accountability partners, etc. I did everything the faith community asked of me and I did it for over three decades. I played by their rules and it caused so much harm. My health broke down, but it meant nothing to them. They did not see that their teaching was hurting me and people around me.

I am healed, not from being gay but from trying to be straight-acting. I got healed, not by getting into the pool at the right time and following the expectations, I got healed when Jesus spoke to me. He said, "Arno, I am not going to heal you, because you are not broken. You have been faithful to your church and your family." That was my Jesus moment. That was my Bethesda Pool moment when God did His thing. It was a different message than I had imagined. It did not conform to the church tradition or my expectations. I did not get healed from being gay, I got healed from shame.

Now, I can pray, enjoy studying the Bible and find the Almighty God within the Scriptures again. There is a fresh desire to minister. I cannot wait to serve at the "temple" once more, because now I know that there is a God who came looking for me, who told me to stand up, and get on with following Jesus. I was a lost sheep within the church flock, but Jesus showed me a new path to life.

Half-time

Matthew 3:13-4:13 (David Bentley Hart Translation)

13 Then Jesus arrived at the Jordan, coming from Galilee to John to be baptised by him.

14 But he prevented him, saying, "I need to be baptised by you, yet you come to me?"

15 But in reply Jesus said to him, "Let me pass now, for it is necessary for us to fulfil every right requirement." Then he lets him pass.

16 And having been baptised, Jesus immediately rose up out of the water, and look: the heavens were opened, and he saw God's Spirit descending as a dove, alighting upon him;

17 And look: a voice out of the heavens, saying, "This is my Son, the beloved, in whom I have delighted."

1 Then Jesus was led up into the wilderness by the Spirit to be tried by the Slanderer.

2 And, having fasted for forty days and forty nights, he was hungry.

3 And, drawing near, the Tempter said to him, "If you are God's Son, command these stones become loaves of bread."

4 He, however, answered by saying, "It has been written, 'The human being shall live not upon bread alone, but upon every utterance issuing from the mouth of God.'"

5 Then the Slanderer carries him off into the Holy City, and stood him upon the pinnacle of the Temple,

6 And says to him, "If you are God's Son, cast yourself down; for it has been written that 'He will command his angels concerning you' and that 'They will catch you in their hands, that you may not strike your foot against a stone.'"

7 "Conversely," said Jesus to him, "it has been written, 'You shall not put the Lord your God to the test.'"

8 Again the Slanderer carries him off, to an extremely high mountain, and displays before him all the kingdoms of the world, and their glory,

9 And said to him, "All of these things I shall give you, were you to prostrate yourself and make obeisance to me."

10 Then Jesus says to him, "Be gone, Accuser: for it has been written, 'You shall make obeisance to the Lord your God and him only shall you adore.'"

11 Then the Slanderer leaves him alone, and look: Angels arrived and ministered to him.

12 Now, hearing that John had been handed over, he withdrew into Galilee.

13 And, departing from Nazareth, he came and took up his dwelling in Capernaum beside the sea...

WHY IS IT that blessing and battle so often go hand in hand? I find it emotionally confusing. How shall I respond? Do I allow myself to be happy, knowing that there are still things to worry about?

I find it draining, and I think I all too often end up focusing, either on the worry-part or the battle-part of my life. Wishing to be honest and transparent, I end up overemphasising what is tough instead of what God has done until now.

I am reminded of the Jesuits who talk about consolation and desolation. They encourage us to really hold on to the times of blessing when feeling consoled, content, and at peace. They believe that these times of comfort can help us get through the tougher times, times of desolation, despair, and emotional isolation, but we need to acknowledge them, and embrace them.

Jesus was on a mission. He had travelled from Galilee to the Jordan river with a purpose. He wanted to get baptised (3:13). Jesus was not just fooling around; at this stage in his life, He had set His face like flint. He was not half-hearted but walked with a single-minded focus. How I love those times, when I just know what to do and I do not let anything stop me. But there are too many times when I am in two minds. I simply do not know the way forward. Sometimes the most difficult thing is to choose between two good options.

At times, I just get so confused when I sense that Jesus is speaking to me. Can it really be true? Is it just my own voice or is it that of Jesus? I often do spiritual journaling. I sit down, ask Jesus to speak to me, and then I start writing in my spiritual journal. I write fast and I try at first not to discern or evaluate what I am writing. But then the discernment phase sets in: All these beautiful thoughts, are they from Jesus or are they just holy wishes and dreams flowing from my own heart? I am not always able to discern that, but I know that I need Jesus.

John the Baptist was also confused about Jesus's request (3:14). Why should John baptise Jesus when He did not have anything to repent of? John was preaching repentance, asking people to get baptised as a sign that they had joined a progressive community of believers. They were baptised into a new reality, where they would choose the ways of the Kingdom instead of the ways of the Romans and society.

Jesus commissioned John to baptise him. It was the wrong way around and John knew it. Jesus can be so confusing. How can we serve Him? We cannot help Him to salvation or repentance, but we can invite Him to join us in our baptism as we become part of His mystical body, the Body of Christ of believers. We join with Him and He joins with us, so we can take part in Him. Jesus invites us to take part in the same journey, the journey towards the cross, and the end of all evil. How big is that!

I have a role to play in the Body of Christ. Like John, I am invited to be involved in this baptism mystery. Jesus gave His body to me and I give my life to Him. Together we become the Body of Christ on earth. We become deified as the Orthodox church calls it. I become one with Christ and become like Christ when I am in Christ. John opened a door for us when he obeyed Jesus. In the same way, we serve Jesus when we help the poor, speak up for the vulnerable, and touch the lives of the people on the margins (Matthew 25:35-36). We are to continue John's ministry of being frontrunners for Jesus.

Jesus is puzzling, because we do not always understand the requirements of the Kingdom and the Kingdom agenda (3:15). We grow up in a world, where our culture educates us about right and wrong and how things are done. Coming to Christ I had to learn and keep on learning lots of new ways to do things.

When I finished my church leadership training with Ichthus Christian Fellowship, we were all given a short, written evaluation. My mentor wrote that I still had a lot to learn about Kingdom leadership. I was schooled in management, but not in ways of the Kingdom. I remember being upset about that comment, but it was spot on. I could lead the church in the way of the latest management theory, but I did not have a clue about the alternative, radical ways of the Kingdom. I hope I am learning otherwise how can I honour God through my leadership?

When baptised, Jesus experienced a new reality. The reality of the spiritual realm: the heavens, the God dimension, or the expanse, opened the door wide enough for Jesus to get a glimpse of what was going on. Heaven and earth were coming together, and the dimensions kissed. God's power and messenger, the Holy Spirit, was on the move and His presence was noticeable (3:16), but not only that: His presence led to a revelation (3:17). God spoke His words of affirmation to Jesus.

Pushing the boundaries of our thinking and experiences of the Divine is a tool in the hands of the Holy Spirit. The Spirit reveals something of God's love to us. It is so special that we are sometimes lost for words.

Here the message is simple, but profound. God the Almighty is crazily in love with Jesus, who is the face of God. In evangelising, we often tell people that God loves them, but I think some people feel that this is just an empty statement. It is not worth their time or consideration. Words have become as cheap as spin, psychological manipulations and the latest psychological techniques have become the norm.

It is quite different, though, when we experience God's presence in our lives, when God is doing something deep within us. At that moment, we know that we are loved. We do not need to convince others. We just know.

I love when others prophecy over me, and I often long for more. Similarly, I know how life changing it has been, when God revealed Himself to me through His word, through prayer or dreams. I can build my life on that. I just know that it is true. I cannot create those moments, and I never know, when they will take place. I just know that when they happen, I think, feel and behave differently as a result.

Think of Mary who kept Divine revelation in her heart (Luke 2:19) or Paul who was shown something impactful in the third heaven (2 Corinthians 12:2). Both let the revelation grow in their lives. Both let it transform their reality and their faith. Revelation gives us the courage to stand. Revelation helps us to have a real and life transforming faith.

I realise that it may not just be Jesus asking confusing things of us. The Holy Spirit is also doing confusing things to us. No wonder that we find spiritual discernment a bit of a challenge. What is of God, what is of the Devil and what might just be circumstantial?

Jesus was sent by the Holy Spirit to a lonely place (4:1). He had experienced a spiritual high, and then He was hit by a period with no rules, no security, and no road map. He had to survive a time in the desert and find God in all the barrenness of life.

We may think that today's world is full of temptations, but the tempter has been around since the fall in the heavens. He is the father of lies, the accuser, and the slanderer. The world is in the hands of the evil one, so he can choose the time and the place, and he will.

As Jesus contemplated His baptism and the revelation of God, He was also confronted with a spiritual trial. Would He be able to stand firm in His faith or would He falter? Could His faith carry Him through, or would He compromise and make short cuts? Only time would tell.

Maybe that is why the Holy Spirit led Him to this half-time in His life: a pause, a break from his daily living, but also a time of extreme loneliness. Would this break lead to a spiritually fulfilling life or would it be His downfall?

I have experienced being thrown into a half-time, a desert time as well. I was sure I was never going to have a midlife crisis; I was all too busy for that! Well, life caught up with me and what was meaningful and joyful, lost its appeal. I think that for many Christians from the LGBT+ communities, the desert time after coming out can be very real. Some of us were thrown into isolation by our families or church communities. Others end up there because we start to re-evaluate our faith in the light of the theology that has hurt us and damaged us. In the wilderness, we must make up our minds. Do we let go of our faith, or are we able to interpret important passages from an inclusive angle even if our friends disagree with us in our conclusions? Can we still love the church, even when the church does not love and embrace us?

The wilderness is very real for some in the LGBT+ communities. The desert speaks loudly and demands an answer. Our lives and our faith are on trial and we may be alone. There are things that can only be solved when alone. Others may care and try to ease the burden, but there are decisions we must make for ourselves. Now is the time to find out if our faith can cope when under attack. The slanderer will use any trick in the book, so are we able to stand when somebody is trying to trip us up? That is what the wilderness is asking of us. Who are you and what do you really believe deep down? That is why it is a spiritual exercise orchestrated by the Holy Spirit.

In our emotional and mental wilderness, we face different challenges. One of them is that we have no idea when this period of our lives will end. Jesus was there for 40 days, but it may take years for some of us. That is my personal experience, and it looks like we sometimes end up there on a number of occasions during our lifetime.

The time is not chosen by us. We are sent into the wilderness. Some of us lose our ministries, family, country, and our friends. What I found difficult is that I do not have a clue now when this time of testing is over. When challenges are prolonged, it is easier to grab hold of the short cuts offered to us, and they will be offered to us. Jesus was offered three.

The first short cut is about having our needs met. Jesus was hungry (4:2-3) and the tempter offered Him a way out: He could just make bread out of the stones. It looked very harmless, and we know that there were times where Jesus prayed, and God provided food for the multitudes. What was different this time? Maybe Jesus did not want to embrace an instant gratification culture of taking anything we want just because we can get away with it. Maybe He did not want to make it all about Him and His needs. This miracle would not glorify God, instead He wanted to trust God for His immediate needs.

As a gay man, am I tempted to have casual sex whenever I feel alone? Am I tempted to apply for any kind of leadership position in society just because I want to regain status after losing my leadership position in the church? Satan will offer us short cuts to make us believe that we can easily have our emotional and mental as well as physical needs met. If the church does not want us, then what is the purpose of living a moral, ethical, and holy life? If we are doomed no matter what, why not enjoy everything that life has in store for us? Let all inhibitions go and let us eat, drink and be happy!

Jesus rejected that line of thinking as He focused on having His needs met by God's revelation (4:4). God alone can feed the deepest needs in our lives and Jesus showed us that it is worth the wait. Hold on to God. He is the lover of our souls and He knows the pain in our hearts. He is the faithful parent who wants to give good gifts to His children. So, hold on.

The second short cut deals with emotional safety. Jesus was encouraged to throw Himself down from the highest point of the Temple (4:5-6). Being gay may create emotional turmoil within ourselves. I hear of many who have tried to change, and done everything the church has asked of them, but the voices of shame, guilt and feeling worthless can be powerful. What do we do to quiet these voices? Some use drink or drugs, others leave their faith, hoping that the condemning voices will disappear.

The tempter tried to make Jesus do crazy things like jumping from a high point. Jesus refused to do the crazy stuff that is neither helping us nor God. Do not test God by asking Him to rescue you from any stupid thought in the spur of the moment, including those that look super spiritual like the one Jesus faced.

Risky behaviour can go wrong, no matter how much God loves us. God has given us a brain and a free will, and we are asked to use it, not to misuse it to prove a point. We may self-destruct in the process. I see LGBT+ Christians who do not hold back after coming out. Their pain is so strong that they want to try and do everything. Sometimes these experiments cause scars on the soul. Jesus did not say that we should not try new things and have new experiences. But He did stop Himself from going overboard just to prove a point.

The final short cut deals with our desires and calling. Jesus was offered all the Kingdoms by the ruler of this world (4:8). It was a good try. Jesus was sent to the world out of love for the world and to take it back from the grip of the enemy. This third temptation dealt with the purpose of His life. He was offered the leadership of the world without facing the cross. Satan offered Him a way out, an easier way to reach His life purpose and mission, but then Jesus would not have put an end to evil.

When I came out, I lost my international ministry and everything I had worked for. It was easy to get angry, bitter, and resentful. Being thrown into years of wilderness did not help either. I had been rejected by the church movement that I had helped found and lead. I was rejected by other evangelical churches. What was I going to do? Do I have a future as a minister of the Word?

For months, nobody wanted me. After getting a job in a Christian organisation, I started to see different possibilities. There were some great leadership positions around that would offer some level of prestige, but it was outside the Christian community. I discerned that this was the false spirit tempting me to compromise as I was frustrated with my job. The option was not a real option because it did not support my calling and mission in life. It would take me away from the Christian community instead of helping me to deepen my involvement in the Christian community and the world.

The tempter's suggestions may look attractive and they may not even be sinful, but they will lead us away from Jesus and a deep and relevant faith.

Jesus was clear. We can only choose options that help us to worship God (4:10). He did not tell us that real Christian living is to work for Christian organisations or do full-time church ministry, but He encouraged us to make choices that honour Him.

Jesus believed that God would make a way, so He did not need to compromise. His life purpose would become a reality. It may take a bit longer than what we would prefer, but it will happen. The Quakers talk about patience as a key indicator when trying to discern God's will. If we do not have the time to let our inkling be tested by others, then it is probably just a human impulse. When we place our hope in God, then we can cope with a bit of waiting time – even though it is hard.

After these three crucial challenges, Jesus finished His alone time. Now, He was ready for fellowship, and the spiritual reality was feeding His soul again (4:11). God had revealed Himself to Him at His baptism. This revelation had taken hold of Him, maybe because He knew the Scriptures well, was used to worship and had a great understanding of God. His faith could hold Him when the going got tough. He came out stronger from this time of solitude and reflection.

His baptism and wilderness experience became a wakeup call to Jesus. As a result, He moved from Nazareth to Capernaum where He began His public ministry (4:12-13). Now He was ready to face the world. May the wilderness times in our lives help the LGBT+ communities to become stronger in faith and in our identity in Christ. We are His beloved, so there is no need to be rebellious or to compromise. It is time to minister to a broken world. May healing flow from our brokenness.

It is for the Best

John 15:1-17 (David Bentley Hart Translation)

1 "I am the true vine and my Father is the husbandman.

2 Every branch in in me that does not bear fruit he takes away; and every branch that bears fruit he trims clean so that it might bear more fruit.

3 You are already clean because of the word I have spoken to you.

4 Remain in me – and I in you. Just as the branch cannot bear fruit from itself unless it remain in the vine, so neither can you unless you remain in me.

5 I am the vine, you are the branches; the one remaining in me and I in him, this one bears plentiful fruit, because apart from me you can do nothing.

6 Unless someone remain in me he is like the branch that has been cast outside and has withered, and they gather them up and cast them in the fire, and they are burned.

7 If you remain in me and my words remain in you, ask whatever you wish, and it shall happen for you.

8 By this my Father has been glorified: that you bear plentiful fruit and will become my disciples.

9 As the Father has loved me I have also loved you; remain in my love.

10 If you keep my commandments, you will remain in my love, just as I have kept my Father's commandments, you will remain in his love.

11 I have spoken these things to you that my joy may be in you and your joy may be made full.

12 This is my commandment: that you love one another as I have loved you.

13 No one has greater love than this: that he should lay down his soul for his friends.

14 You are my friends if you do what I command you.

15 I call you slaves no longer, because the slave does not know what his lord is doing; but I have called you friends, because everything I have heard from the Father I have made known to you.

16 You did not choose me, but I chose you and appointed you, so that you should go and should bear fruit, and your fruit will last, so that whatever you might ask in my name he might give you.

17 These things I command you so that you love one another."

How beautiful it is to see the relationship between the Almighty God and Jesus (15:1). They interact so that everything is in harmony. They are in a loving relationship where one honours the other. I see Jesus as this wonderful vine. It is healthy, it is beautiful, and it is ripe. He is just so ready, and still the Father is helping Him to become more fruitful. He is the tree of life, all the food we need for the journey towards God.

I am part of that tree, in the same way as I am part of the Body of Christ (15:2). I was baptised into the Body and was grafted into the tree. Can it get any better? My life is about fellowship. Fellowship with the Godman Jesus and fellowship with all the other body parts or branches, or whatever beautiful picture we can think of. It speaks to me about community, the community of saints. These saints are pilgrims who are exploring what life with God is all about.

I notice that when I am part of this fellowship, then God is not just working on Jesus, He is also working on my life. I am not always sure what is happening. I can identify with being cut down. I lost many things within 48 hours of coming out. It was so unfair, and it hurt so much. I guess that any pruning or cutting down hurts and I could not discern the difference. I could only notice the pain and the unfairness. I had served faithfully for 18 years in another country and now it was all over. Nobody wanted me. There were no church jobs available to somebody like me anymore, and the secular world did not respond to my job applications. I was out, cut off, cut down. Where to look, where to turn?

I thought it was all the work of the Devil and maybe it was, but what if God was using the situation? What if God was using even an un-fair situation to trim me for His glory? Maybe God was using all the things that happened to me and my family so that we may bear more fruit? Maybe he helped take away all the things that so easily entangle and hold me/us back? And maybe, just maybe He also pruned certain aspects of my life to enable the more fruitful sides of my life to become even more fruitful? What if these years of ministry were a false start? Maybe there is something so much better to come when God gets the chance to really work on my life through His Spirit. Maybe I just need to learn to surrender, to love, and to follow His lead?

I am clean (15:3)! What a statement. I am clean. My mind has been cleansed from all the filthy, hurtful words that have been spoken over me as a gay man throughout my life. All the things that were said directly to me or indirectly through TV, sermons, books and just people discussing "the gays." God's word can cleanse me from all the wrongdoing of others, so my mind does not keep on working overtime dissecting the unfairness: "He said, she said." I do not need to make sense of it all. I do not need to know their motives and intentions. God has set me free. His Word, Jesus, has set me free from all the thoughts, anger, and bitterness. The words of Jesus are the healing balm for my soul and thought life.

But Jesus is not only cleansing me from the sins committed against me, but also from the sins I committed when I missed the mark of who God created me to be. I need to stand strong in my identity. I am sinning against God when conforming to the patterns of this world (Romans 12:2). I cannot minister, love, and work with impact when I am half-hearted because I cannot put my whole being into the situation. Hiding and pretending does not glorify God. If I want to walk on the road towards God, then I must do it the Jesus way. I can and must embrace God's creation. I am not just connected to the tree of life, I am part of the tree of life when I choose to follow Him.

Jesus, keep on speaking your revelation into my life! Do not keep quiet, help me to see, help me to hear, help me to follow. I want to be sustained by you and not by pulling myself together and trying to please church traditions and cultural norms. I am cleansed because of Jesus, so my conscience is clear.

Salvation means remaining in Jesus, following Jesus (15:4). In my evangelical tradition, we ask if people have received Jesus into their hearts. I have noticed that the Bible is more focused on followership. Do I follow Jesus? Am I doing the Jesus stuff or am I just proclaiming something that does not have a real influence on my priorities and values in life?

I need to remain, to stay connected to the tree of life, to my Jesus, my Saviour. I see a picture of a baby in the mother's womb. Her life is the baby's life. Her nutrition will feed the baby. I am a baby in Christ's womb together with all my other siblings in the faith. We live in Christ and He lives through us. We become one with Him, adopted into His family.

I can feel safe like the baby in the womb when I let go of all my hurries and worries. When I let go of all the conflicting voices in my mind and I listen for the One voice: The heartbeat of my Jesus. It makes me safe. I can hear Him; I hear the sound and the words that I know so well, and they calm my troubled mind.

Why is it that I think I can do things on my own? Why do I sometimes get so big headed that I lose the heartbeat, the sound of my Saviour's voice, and His touch? That wonderful touch of Jesus when He fills me with His presence, His love, His peace, and His joy. Those moments, they are Divine.

You are right. I am useless without Christ. Then I just do life on my own. I know the church has mistreated me and others like me, but maybe we need some new wine skins. Maybe, instead of walking away from church, worship and fellowship, I am called to create church, worship and fellowship. Maybe that is one of the ways in which I can pass on that cleansing that I have experienced.

I really do believe that the world needs Jesus. I cannot save, heal, deliver, prophecy, feed the thousands, but God can. I cannot heal my own wounds and find self-acceptance without the words of Jesus. I cannot overcome body-shaming without hearing His voice that reveals to me that I am also wonderfully made and fully His. When He says that my body is good, then why do I think it is rubbish? In those moments, I have surrendered by listening to the false spirit instead of the Spirit of Truth. Even though I was asked to leave the church, it is my responsibility to find another place, another body of believers, as I am still part of the mystical, universal Body of Christ. I need the power and the truth to help me against all those distorting voices, since they will not stop, just because I turn my back on the church that turned its back on me when I needed it the most.

So much talent goes to waste (15:6). People who are in the wrong jobs, wrong relationships, or wrong faith communities. Throughout history women were told that they could not work, lead, or minister. Slaves were told that they were subhuman. Dalits are told that they are hated by God. Gays are told that we are an abomination and on the fast train to hell.

How come that we are so keen on putting other people down and pushing them out of relationship? How come we do not believe that we are all created in God's image and therefore we have a responsibility? We have a calling to God's world; we are called to gather.

I have been pastoring. I worked long days, and all too often I felt that God was just a hard taskmaster. At times, there was little joy in the ministry, only long hours, and commitments. I was too busy working for God to waste time with God. I did have prayer times, but they were long lists of needs for the ministry, for my family or all the sick people in need of healing from God. In many ways they were all important things, but they still took me away from my first love for God. Faith had become a business arrangement, and a very unhealthy one.

I do not want to go to waste just because the church tells me that I can no longer be a pastor because I am gay. I have found that it does not really matter if I am celibate or in a relationship. The denominations that I know, do not queue up to employ a gay pastor, no matter what.

What do I do? I do not want to wither away, be gathered up and cast into the fire. I will choose to follow the voice of Jesus. He tells me that I am clean. He tells me that I need to be sustained by Him and remain in His love. I choose to stay with Jesus and find the people of Jesus who also have a heart for people like me. People who will look at the fruit of my life and not only my sexual orientation.

How easy it is to lose the revelation that Jesus has spoken into my life (15:7). I hear other people's voices loud and clear, so the whispers of Jesus can sometimes be put on mute or forgotten. People's opinions and my own thoughts can be extremely persuasive. I do not always notice when I move towards a spiritual and emotional desert. I just feel a bit tired, need time for myself, sulk a bit, and eat some more chocolate! But the words of Jesus, those freeing words of Jesus are life giving.

If I hold on to my passions and the words of Jesus, then I have something positive and constructive to pray about. Then I become a visionary. Then I hope for change, because Jesus is my hope. I am no longer begging God to love somebody enough to heal them. I do not need to convince God that I desperately long for a boyfriend. He knows. But what I can do is to trust that His words are more real and heartfelt, and they can create true transformation in my life.

Prayer times, times of contemplation and Bible meditation can become food for the soul. When wasting time with God, I become a more integrated person. I become whole as He infuses me with His Spirit, and I gain new life from the tree of life. He is like a blood transfusion or a river of life.

Doing ministry in South Asia as well as in Europe has been eye-opening. In India many of the believers in our churches would pray, read the Bible, and take part in prayer and fasting days. In Denmark and England on the other hand, attending church a couple of times a month was perceived as being committed. People tell me that "it is important not to become fanatical and we all have so much to do"; but becoming disciples and bearing fruit is God's heart for us (15:8). Believing in God is not enough, believing in the cross and the resurrection is not enough, speaking in tongues is not enough. God is asking us to bear fruit, to be sustained by Him, to be filled with His Words and let them transform our lives. He is asking us to follow Him.

There is a richness in our faith that we so easily lose. We accept so many demands on our lives, that God is being squeezed out. Our faith becomes lifeless and loveless, but I cannot stand as a gay man and bear fruit without God and fellowship. I know myself too well. Without God, I will just become a career junkie. I will go for the limelight, I will try to build an image, but then I might just as well go back into the closet again.

Instead of image making and image management, it is time for authentic living, so God can be glorified. I do not have the energy to keep up with the Joneses in the church anymore. When I tried my best, I was an accepted pastor, but I often wondered if people would love me for who I am if they knew the fuller version of me? Would they love me when they knew my secret, you know, the gay thing?

The question kept on eating at me, and then I found out. Some people could not get their heads around me being gay and they just turned their backs on me or stayed silent. It was a hard lesson, but it was also filled with good surprises. There were people who appreciated me for who I am. They could still see the love, the commitment, and the fruit of my faith and ministry.

So how can we ensure that we are not wasting our lives when rejected? For me, I focus on being a follower of Christ and on gathering with likeminded Christians.

I have a calling on my life, and it is my responsibility to be faithful to God despite the challenges. Other people, including the church, do not get to decide if I shall be allowed to glorify God or not. Any real blessing will only grow out of my relationship with Him who grafted me into the tree of life, so I will choose to stick with Him.

Divine Appointments

Luke 10:25-37 (David Bentley Hart Translation)

25 And Look: A certain lawyer stood up to test him, saying, "Teacher, by what deed may I inherit life in the Age?"

26 And he said to him, "What has been written in the Law? How do you read it?"

27 And in reply he said, "You shall love the Lord your God out of the whole of your heart and in the whole of your soul and in the whole of your strength and in the whole of your mind, and you neighbour as yourself."

29 But he, wishing to vindicate himself, said to Jesus, "And who is my neighbour?"

30 Taking this up, Jesus said, "A certain man was going down from Jerusalem, and he fell among bandits, who stripped him and rained blows upon him and went away leaving him half dead.

31 And by a coincidence a certain priest was going down by that road and, seeing him, passed by on the opposite side.

32 And a Levite also, coming upon the place and seeing him, passed by on the opposite side.

33 But a certain Samaritan on a journey came upon him and was inwardly moved with compassion,

34 And approaching bandaged his wounds, pouring on oil and wine, and setting him upon his own mount he brought him to a lodge and cared for him.

35 And taking out two denarii on the following day he gave them to the keeper of the lodge and said, "Take care of him, and whatever you spend beyond this I shall repay you on my return."

36 Who of these three does it seem to you became a neighbour to the man falling among bandits?"

37 And he said, "The one treating him with mercy." And Jesus said to him, "Go and do likewise."

TESTING? I AM not sure I like that word (10:25). How can anybody do their best work under pressure? How can you stay calm and answer in the right spirit when the other person wants you to fail? Maybe having somebody looking over your shoulder is not the most conducive way to produce great results.

From my own life, I can also think of all too many times, when I became defensive, felt that people were testing or questioning my integrity, my faith, or the quality of my work. Those tense situations can kick start our defence mechanisms and I know that one as a gay man.

Many things became a test while living in the closet. How to make sure nobody noticed when I found another man attractive. How to ensure that I would not have a Freudian slip of the tongue, so people might be able to guess my secret.

I remember inviting many people from the church to the theatre to watch a Motown show. The performers dressed and danced like the old famous singers. At some point, the Master of Ceremonies was encouraging all the ladies to shout for the upcoming act, The Temptations. He introduced some greatly attractive men, so I cheered, thinking that he would announce that we should also cheer for some female performers. That never happened, so I was cheering away for the hunky men and some of my female church members turned around and looked at me! I was so embarrassed. I was not out to my church, and I had let my guard down for a moment. I did not pass the test and I could not do anything about it except look as if I were just enjoying the performance, hoping that people would not take my cheering too seriously.

Closeted people often live under a lot of stress as I did. It was hard work having to suppress thoughts and emotions and reject aspects of my identity. I always had to consider which books I could read and which TV programmes I could watch that would not be too revealing.

I had to consider how to answer pastoral questions and theological dilemmas with great care. There were also lots of little things like what clothes to wear, if my gestures were too camp, how to explain why I did not enjoy football, where to look and what to say. It was exhausting living in the closet and only being myself when I was on my own. That could easily develop into an interesting internet search history! All the things I wanted to research, often at unsociable hours and without anybody knowing, made me more unsociable, tired and disintegrated.

The theological scholar in the story asked an important question and I guess that some LGBT+ Christians are just as interested in the answer. Do we stand a chance in the Age to come, will we be saved?

Rarely do sermons send us into heaven, more commonly to everlasting damnation. This creates fear and anger within our LGBT+ communities and there are people who leave the church as a result. Some parents of LGBT+ children may also fear for the eternal destination of their LGBT+ child. They love their child, but fear for their salvation. What to do?

But what about me? Do I stand a chance? Am I reading the Bible in a way that fits my longings? Am I trying to get a cheap ticket into heaven and continue what some people call sinful behaviour?

The more generous Christians tell me that my salvation is secure if I stay celibate, but if I become a "practising homosexual," then my salvation will be under threat. Isn't it only natural for me, then, to ask God what deed I can do to stay saved just like the scholar (10:25)? If I will lose my salvation because of a deed, then there must be an antidote, another deed, that I can do to stay saved now and for eternity.

I wonder what Jesus might do or say. Will he tell me that I just pick and mix Scripture to serve my purpose like some of my Christian friends or will He have a different approach?

I will enter the text and meditate on it to see how the passage relates to my life and we begin with Jesus responding with two questions, *"What has been written in the Law? How do you read it?"* (10:26)

My mind was racing. He knew that I had been a pastor for many years, so it should be an easy question, but not for me. My own life and that of the LGBT+ communities were hanging in the balance. It matters what I said and how Jesus responded. I would either be liberated or condemned.

My spiritual family says that the deed is clear: Stay celibate. That is the only way for gay Christians. If not, I will lose my salvation. There is therefore only one deed. The deed of abstaining from a deed! I will be saved by what I do not do.

In the end I just blurted it out. I referred to the way Jewish people sum up their faith (10:27). We need to love God with our whole be-ing and other people too. The 'other people' bit, is quite hard though.

Does the Bible truly teach that I must love the straight Christians who hurt me and my family but at the same way, do they have to love me to be saved?

How far can we stretch this concept of love because there must surely be boundaries? At least, that is what people say who are against LGBT+ Christians in the church, in leadership positions, (no matter if we have a partner or not), etc.

I had to hear the answer directly from Jesus because my salvation depended on it. I needed to get it right as I have been searching for that answer for decades. I have been told that the Bible is clear about gay Christians, gay marriage, etc, and for many years I just took it for granted without checking it for myself. I have realised that I cannot put that responsibility on other people's shoulders. I need to know what salvation is about. It is too important for me to outsource to other church leaders and allow tradition to make demands on my life and my happiness.

I asked Jesus about those other people that I needed to love, my neighbours (10:29). He answered with a story. The story was very personal to me because I recognised much of the story from my own life story. As He told the story, I could feel it, see it, remember it. I saw the faces of the people; I felt it in my gut. I got a bit nervous as I did not want to go back and revisit the pain. I look for trauma healing, not to be retraumatised. Jesus was wise. He knew what I needed to hear, and only by engaging with reality would I be able to change - and - heal.

In the story a man was returning from Jerusalem, the place of worship and I was that man walking alone (10:30). I had been a pastor for 18 years in the same town. I knew it well. I knew many people, had engaged with many different organisations, churches, and institutions over the years.

Coming out was a lonely journey and I also met some bandits on my way. They were some of my friends who had known my story for years.

We shared our decision to divorce with our fellow leaders and within 48 hours they stripped us of our ministry in the church. We were already vulnerable as a family as we were trying to find our feet and answers to a lot of practical questions, e.g. housing, finances, etc. We did not get the chance to tell our story. Other people decided to out us. To me it was spiritual and emotional abuse and we did not get any closure.

I can identify with the man in the story left for dead. I was thrown out like litter; used and thrown away. Everything I/we had done as a family over the years, what we had invested in people's lives, did not matter. I was emotionally stripped of my dignity and of my international ministry. I could not make heads or tails of what was going on.

Jesus had not finished the story though. He told me about a man, a priest, who passed by, but chose to walk around me (10:31). He did not check up on me, ask me any questions. It was as if I did not exist and he did not know me.

I do not recall receiving any phone calls from any pastor colleagues. I knew so many of them, but none of them showed any interest. I learnt a lesson about pastoral care or the lack of it. How I longed for a phone call or somebody asking if we could meet for a cuppa. I learnt that leadership and suffering can be a very lonely place.

Jesus did not let allow me dwell on the pain, accusations, and disappointments. He moved the story on. He talked about a Levite who was copying the behaviour of the priest (10:32). It is amazing how church members notice what we do more than what we say. When pastors and leaders do not show support to somebody, then why should the church members? Would it be acceptable for them to show

care for us and for me if the leaders did not? Many church members and friends also chose to give us the silent treatment. Maybe they did not know what to do or what to say? Maybe they were coloured by the announcement given in the church?

I wondered about all the people that we had helped over the years. I wondered about our co-pastors in other countries. One co-pastor said to me, "Everybody wants you as their friend, but nobody wants you as their leader." That hurt. He also went dark for months and later told me it was to teach me a lesson. I am not sure what lesson that was, except that I should not expect Christian friends and colleagues to stand with me when hurting and humiliated.

It was such a lonely and painful place. Some days I was extremely angry, while at other times I was despondent. I could only beg for God's mercy.

Jesus did it again. He did not allow me to dwell on my pain and my self-pity for too long. He continued the story. There was also a third person. The surprising one. The one who did not fit the story line. We started with the priest, then the Levite and then it should have been a fellow Jew. But Jesus does not colour within the lines. He pushes boundaries, so we are forced to think a bit deeper.

The third person was the Samaritan man (10:33). The outsider who did not fit the picture just like Jesus never fitted the picture. This person came from another region and another ethnic group. In the story, he became the answer to the pain, and he took the initiative to start the healing process.

I experienced that too. There were two weeks left until we had to empty the house and move out. I had nowhere to go. I had been dismissed from my ministry and I had no income. I did not even get any benefits from the government. I was getting desperate. There was a referendum in the UK and the majority voted for Brexit. I was fed up with that result too. The campaign had been extremely negative, and people from the EU like me were getting the blame for many things. Hate crimes increased. For the first time I wondered if it was time for me to return to Denmark. I had nowhere to live, but maybe I could get a job. I had tried for some time in the UK without luck.

I wrote to an English couple who were ministering in Copenhagen at the time. We knew each other and ministered together years ago in the UK. I told them about the divorce, my life story, etc. They wrote back and told me that I could come and stay with them. They were pastors, and national leaders of a church denomination that does not have an affirming theology regarding LGBT+ Christians. They invited me to their home. I could live there, eat their food, and start my journey towards recovery. They loved me, they listened to me, my hurt, and my pain. They were Jesus to me just like the good Samaritan was Jesus to the man in pain.

This couple was the surprising neighbour that in many ways should not be in support of me. They were ethnically different, they came from another region/nation, and they were leaders in a non-affirming denomination. They could get into trouble for housing me, but they did it and we became family. When I could stand on my own two feet, they got a new appointment in another country! Talk about God's timing.

They were moved with compassion like the Samaritan and embraced me like a brother. Their compassion was greater than any theological concerns or concerns about their reputation. They saw a brother in need and that was enough for them.

I was so relieved. The story was no longer just about pain, sorrow, and trauma. It was not a sweet story either. It was a story with twists and turns, a real story just like mine.

Jesus did not finish there though. I had asked Him what to do and Jesus gave me yet another challenge to think about. He asked me to consider who was the true neighbour in this story. That was, of course, the Samaritan, or in my life, my English friends (10:36-37).

I had enjoyed their hospitality in a time of need, and then Jesus asked me to be the same kind of friend to others (10:37).

I am reminded of the theological scholar in the story. When Jesus answered that he, too, was expected to love others, common thinking would be that he should only love fellow Jews. It would have been a great surprise to him that he was asked to behave like the foreigner.

The story challenges me. How can I show love to non-affirming church groups that condemn me? How can I be Jesus to people who see things differently to me and who put up barriers for my life and ministry?

In the same way as I have experienced love and compassion, it is now my responsibility to do the same to others, especially those I disagree with.

But what about my salvation deed? I sit back with great joy in my heart. My salvation is not depending on the things that I do not do; if I have a relationship with another man or not, but on my love for Christ. My salvation is based on loving God and taking initiative to show loving deeds to others even those that I disagree with. I just need to follow in the footsteps of Jesus and then I am on my Way.

The Cage of Despair

Psalm 121 (The Passion Translation)

1-2 I look up to the mountains and hills, longing for God's help. But then I realise that our true help and protection come only from the Lord, our Creator who made the heavens and the earth.

3 He will guard and guide me, never letting me stumble or fall. God is my Keeper; he will never forget or ignore me.

4 He will never slumber nor sleep; he is the Guardian-God for his people, Israel.

5 Jehovah himself will watch over you; He's always at your side to shelter you safely in his presence.

6 He's protecting you from all danger both day and night.

7 He will keep you from every form of evil or calamity as he continually watches over you.

8 You will be guarded by God himself. You will be safe when you leave your home and safely you will return. He will protect you now, and he'll protect you forevermore!

I WAS WALKING THE streets day after day. I had moved to Copenhagen, Denmark after 18 years in the UK.

I was no longer a tourist; now I was a citizen again, but I was also an alien. It was my country, but it was not my country. I had changed

over the years and so had my country of origin. There were even lots of expressions that were new to me and they sounded weird to my ears.

I had no job, no income, no church, but some friends had offered me a room where I could stay. Friends who were there for me at this extremely challenging time. They were not intrusive, they did not push me, they just cared for me. Our years of history together as fellow Christian leaders made us feel safe in each other's company. We respected and acknowledged God's work in each other's lives; the spiritual journey, the walk with God, and our ministry for God. I had a spiritual home with them.

But I would be in the streets walking and praying each day for hours. I left the house to see the world around me. I had to relearn what Denmark was all about and I desperately needed God's grace, blessing, and healing. I needed God to be my breakthrough because I could not make it on my own. There were simply too many closed doors. Opportunity did not knock on my door.

Over and over, I prayed the first verse of this Psalm as I was prayer walking the streets of Copenhagen. I prayed, *"I lift my eyes to the hills. From where shall my help come?"* (Psalm 121:1, English Standard Version). I needed to learn to trust God. I knew I would probably look in all the wrong places, so I had to remind myself of the truth in this Psalm. God would be the answer to my suffering and my prayer.

When in despair, it is easy to look elsewhere, rather than to God. Here the author looks to the hills or the mountains. Maybe the answer came from there. In Old Testament times there were religious beliefs that certain gods would inhabit the hills while others inhabited the valleys. They believed that they would win a battle if it took place in the area where their god reigned.

We can look to people, institutions, churches, friends, and governments, but ultimately, we need the creative solutions from our Creator.

God will use natural means to solve the problems, but the Almighty is the one encouraging people and organisations to do new things. I worked on believing that the Creator God would come up with a solution. That He would move heaven and earth, so I would not be a waste of space. I knew that only God could turn evil into something good. He has the transforming power to touch the deepest areas of our lives, our emotions, our thinking, our gut reactions, and our fears. Nobody but God can heal the hurts, and God can turn these experiences into something beautiful. Such is the transformative power and reality of the Spirit.

In praying this Psalm, I was reminded of God's love for me, for the individual: He guards, and He guides. I may feel that He is far away, but I am in His presence (121:3). He does not forget or ignore us even when we feel that the world is doing exactly that. But it is hard to realise, that it does not mean that God solves everything immediately. There are things to be done in the spirit world and in the physical world and He does not force people to do anything. He makes His move as a great chess player, but it is up to us how to respond to His moves.

Sometimes I worried if I was going mad. Would I be able to cope with all this rejection and insecurity? And what about the timing? Would it be over soon, or would it take weeks or months? Trying to survive without knowing when change would come was tough. People often say that God will respond in the eleventh hour, but I was living on borrowed money. It was way past midnight. Some of these Christian catch phases are cute, but not very helpful in times of trial – and they are not always that Biblical either.

I felt that God was saying to me that He had to align certain things first before I would experience the breakthrough. The picture He was using in my imagination came from the Disney version of Hercules, where something would happen when several stars were aligned of serving me. He would add extra rolls in my bag or give me some cakes that I like for free. He would make a few jokes or just offer me a smile. He was God sent, so I went to the bakery every day. A stranger would light up my day. How great is that.

Just after returning to Denmark, I read about a short course to become an LGBT Ambassador. It was just two evenings, so I thought I would go. I met the lecturer at the local LGBT+ cafe shortly after the course finished and he invited me home to visit him and his boyfriend. They just wanted to bless me and see if they could help me with ideas for a job. Some months later, they invited me to celebrate Christmas with them and some of their friends. God sends angels to us in all kinds of disguises. My role is to notice what God is doing. This is part of His plan to protect me day and night. He was sending people to lift my spirit in different ways. I was not left alone. A lot of strangers cared for me.

When hurting, I wonder if we add fuel to the fire. In this emotionally desolate place, we may lose objectivity, being in a stressful state of fight, flight, or freeze. We so want to get out of this stressful situation, that we may compromise, make hurried decisions, or try to reduce the distress through establishing unhealthy habits. Will I be able to trust God to keep me from disaster as He journeys with me (121:7)? You will know from my behaviour what I believe. Do I run away from the pain or do I embrace it, trusting that God will watch over me? Do I believe that I must have all the answers, or that God will embrace me and pave the way for me?

I know that I cannot be passive. I must apply for jobs and I applied for many jobs that did not have my interest, but I was desperate for an income. It was hard emotionally to apply for jobs that I did not have my interest at all, that were in parts of the country, where I would probably never feel at home, and that had nothing to do with my calling. How does calling fit into it in times of trouble? Would I be disobeying God by taking a job that was far from my calling or could I serve God in all circumstances, even the ones that were not ideal? I prayed and reflected, reflected and prayed until I was so emotionally raw that I could not think straight anymore. The answer did come through a job opportunity with a Christian organisation. God did watch over me. It was not my dream job, but I was back in a Christian organisation. It was a step in the right direction.

God's protection is a weird concept (121:8). We all know of people who have lost their lives, who go hungry to bed, or who did not find the spouse of their dreams. Life rarely works out the way we expect. So where is God when we really need Him? I am learning through this experience, from these months of prayer walking the streets of Copenhagen, that we are not in control of our lives, but we can put our hope in the God who will never leave us nor forsake us. He is with us in our coming and going; things may go wrong on this journey, but God is there too. And when things go wrong, still nothing can separate us from the love of God. The Devil may separate us from our family and friends, our church, and our community, but God is always there. The church may tell you that God is far away from you because you are gay, but God will never leave you nor forsake you. Your family may turn their backs on you, but God will never leave you nor forsake you.

God will be with us now and in the world to come. He is not going away, and that is what helped me in my cage of despair. He invited me to take steps out of the cage little by little. He showed me a world, a bigger world than I had seen before, including my experience of church. He gave me new friends and new opportunities. He even gave me ministry opportunities in places that are anti-LGBT.

I realise that this is just the start of a new journey. I still need to re-mind myself that my focus is important. Do I look to the mountains, the key players, for an answer, or do I look to the Creator God? I am reminded that, *some trust in chariots and some in horses, but we trust in the name of the LORD our God* (Psalm 20:7, New International Version). When in pain, where do I put my trust? When insecure, where do I find my peace? When in doubt, where do I find faith, hope, and love? The answer will determine my future. I will attempt to put my trust in the God who created the heavens and the earth.

Things Will Change

Jeremiah 29:4-14 (English Standard Version)

4 *"Thus says the LORD of hosts, the God of Israel, to all the exiles whom I have sent into exile from Jerusalem to Babylon:*

5 *Build houses and live in them; plant gardens and eat their produce.*

6 *Take wives and have sons and daughters; take wives for your sons, and give your daughters in marriage, that they may bear sons and daughters; multiply there, and do not decrease.*

7 *But seek the welfare of the city where I have sent you into exile, and pray to the LORD on its behalf, for in its welfare you will find your welfare.*

8 *For thus says the LORD of hosts, the God of Israel: Do not let your prophets and your diviners who are among you deceive you, and do not listen to the dreams that they dream,*

9 *for it is a lie that they are prophesying to you in my name; I did not send them, declares the LORD.*

10 *"For thus says the LORD: When seventy years are completed for Babylon, I will visit you, and I will fulfil to you my promise and bring you back to this place.*

11 *For I know the plans I have for you, declares the LORD, plans for welfare and not for evil, to give you a future and a hope.*

12 *Then you will call upon me and come and pray to me, and I will hear you.*

*13 You will seek me and find me, when you seek me with all
your heart.*

*14 I will be found by you, declares the LORD, and I will restore
your fortunes and gather you from all the nations and all the
places where I have driven you, declares the LORD, and I will
bring you back to the place from which I sent you into exile.*

I AM IN A ministry-exile. Life is quite ok, I have a meaningful job in
many ways, but deep down my longing for something else is strong.
I look over my shoulders, longing for some of the things I did before.
Maybe I am just painting parts of my past in rosy colours, forgetting
the battles and the realities of church ministry, but the longing is
there. I just cannot wait until the day when I can take people on a
spiritual journey, when we can wrestle with Scripture together, and
create an authentic, rooted, and beautiful church community. The
longing is so overwhelming that I feel a deep sense of loneliness due
to restlessness. I feel like bursting with impatience. I have a calling
and a sense of need for teaching the Scriptures, but I am set aside at
least for now.

The Israelites were also set aside. They were expelled from their land
and their everyday life (29:4). They had listened to a prophet who had
only proclaimed good news, but it was not God news. People had
listened to what they would like to hear, but the words did not come
from the heart of God.

Sometimes people tell me that God protects Christians from all evil,
economic troubles and sickness if we put on the full armour of God
or proclaim the blood of Jesus every morning. When in need, these
kinds of promises sound too good to be true, and they are. God has
never promised us a life without challenges, quite the opposite in fact.
I would like to be without fear of illness, and it would be fantastic

living a life without financial problems. When our reality is different, it may be tempting to start believing this kind of success teaching, but there is no magic bullet, or prayer, or lifestyle. Do you recognise the feeling of not being spiritual enough or worry if you are too sinful when things do not go as we learnt from the sermons?

The Israelites were exiled by the Lord for a purpose and so am I. I am on a healing journey, taken out of my normal habitat, so I can get healed from the cynicism that I feel, the bitterness, the trauma, and get a new start with God.

Moving to another country was a big step, even though it was back to my native country after 18 years. I must depend on God for my life in new ways. My life was rebooted at the age of 51! I long for a church ministry, but God is placing me away from the pressure of everyday life in church leadership. I get the chance to preach and teach in different church settings and ministries, but I do not have to face the music day in and day out. God pressed pause, so I could heal. I do not like being on ministry-leave, but God knows what I need more than I do. I am unrealistic in my expectations of myself; during this time my longings are growing, along with my discontent!

The Israelites were told to settle down (29:5). This was a time to build and plant. They were asked to unpack their suitcases literally, but also in their attitude. This exile may take time. They wanted immediate solutions, but God said "stay."

In my own life I do not know how long this phase will be, but God says, "unpack, settle down." I do not want to unpack and settle down. I want a different ministry, a different focus, a new home, and a part-ner. All the things that mean something to me are gone. They were left behind when I was sent into ministry-exile. I wonder when I can pick up the rod and the staff again, but God is asking me to enjoy the present. Plant as if I were never to go back. Get my home in order, so I like being at home. Write the books that are on my heart and explore what God is doing, especially within the Christian LGBT+ communities in different countries.

I want to hear a different message, but God is asking me to get my stress under control. I cannot be effective in ministry before my stress, my hurts, and my painful experiences are laid at the altar.

My future lies in the hands of God as Jesus is the Way, but I am responsible for following Jesus today. And Jesus is saying stay, make the most of it and become fruitful.

The Israelites were asked to get spouses and have children. They needed to trust God enough to make themselves vulnerable. They were to have children, to care for the little ones, while being in hostile territory. Nothing has changed. We are still to be fruitful and multiply by having spiritual children. We do not put our spirituality on hold just because we are excluded from our past ministry. We are to make the most of every situation and therefore we are to invest our lives in others, so that they may see God and follow the Way. I may be on church leadership sabbatical, but I am still expected to have spiritual children. Therefore, I teach, and I preach when possible, and lead a Bible study. I sense God is asking me to behave like a pastor (without a congregation!) by leading people towards the Way: Talk about the things I am learning about God's love and grace. They are deep and impactful lessons as they are transforming me.

When you feel like an alien, a fish out of water, then it is easy to develop an unhelpful attitude towards life: I am just surviving now, and real life starts sometime in the future. It is hard for me to live for today especially when I am unsure about my future. I need a light, a direction to follow, but I only know that I am to be a shepherd, train leaders, write books, and preach. I have no idea where, how, and when. I am tempted to live in the future, dream about the future and lose the blessings of today. I may enjoy things that happen at work or in church, but I minimise them, because I am not in the right ministry, relationship or home yet.

God was asking the Israelites to work and pray for the welfare of the community where they were living in exile (29:7). They were not to use their energy to focus on their return, pray for Jerusalem or how life will be after the exile. They were to focus on being a real blessing right here, right now in their exile. When their communities were being blessed, they were blessed in return. When they did not work for the welfare of their city, then they were robbing themselves of a blessing from God. My life is never about me alone, but about the community and me. When I invest in my community even if it is not a place where I would prefer to be, then it does something to my attitude, and I bless the people around me in the process.

It is astonishing. God was asking them to pray for a positive outcome for a nation that the Jews did not like. You and I may not like our present job, home, relationships, or church, but God is asking us to pray and work for welfare, prosperity, and success everywhere we go. We are to impact others with God's Kingdom now. Why we are in that specific situation or predicament, is less relevant. We may have been sent there, ordered there or because we had no choice, but God says "settle down" because this is not a holiday. Work, pray, and bless the people around you. We are to be little Christ, Christians, wherever we go. We lose out on so many opportunities to minister in the power of God when we get grumpy and restless like me.

Lord, help us, help me in your mercy to rest in your presence, knowing that you know best. Help us, help me to follow you and trust you with our futures, because you are the Way, the Truth, and the Life.

When we are desperate, it is easy to give up on our Christian faith, especially if church has been an upsetting experience. I guess that some of us in the LGBT+ communities have had traumatic experiences in church. We have been asked to leave, been humiliated, outed, refused communion, asked to step down from ministry positions or told we cannot take up any leadership positions, we have been called all kinds of names and told that we are going to hell because of "the lifestyle that we have chosen!"

Therefore, we may be tempted to listen to any voice that gives us some level of hope (29:8-9). I see Christians who leave the church, leave their passionate faith to become critical of everything they believed in the past. I see Christians who try different spiritual practises of other religions in their hunger for a positive faith and a healing spirituality. God asked the Israelites to discern. They needed to discern if what they were paying attention to came from the true spirit or the false spirit. In their hope for change, they would follow anything that sounded like good news, but it would not be the voice of God.

I believe that developing spiritual discernment is critical for any Christian. We need to take our faith journey very seriously and find Christian spiritual mentors and directors who can guide us to a deeper faith. A faith that will hold us even in times of trouble. A theology that is truly good news for minority groups, oppressed groups, and under-represented groups. A theology that does not promise a life without problems, but a faith that is relevant also during times of suffering.

When the time is right, God will bring us out of exile (29:10). We can trust the prophecies and callings that are upon our lives. The Israelites had to wait 70 years to see them fulfilled, so I can hold on to a God who will be working behind the scenes making things right. God is a God of promise. God's dreams are often so big that they extend beyond our lifetime, but that does not mean that God is not going to do something through you and me now. He will use us so that the world will know that there is a loving God. He will bring us out, He will bring us home. We will be free, liberated. I do believe that.

Nelson Mandela is reported to have said that it was a good thing that he was in prison for 27 years, otherwise he would not have become a president of reconciliation. He was not ready before then.

At a time in history, God will bring us out of our ministry-exile. He will bring us to that home where we can live and love. The place where we feel safe maybe for the first time in our lives. We dare to take risks, because we are grounded in ourselves and God.

Then we come to a famous verse that is often taken out of context. I have heard of churches passing it on as a promise verse at New Year celebrations. However, the verse is stating that God has a beautiful dream for us, though not immediately, but after a time in exile (29:11). We cannot just tell our fellow believers that God has a plan and a hope for our future without evil and challenges. God is saying that after the troubles, then we will experience a true blessing. God does not want evil to get a hold on us and therefore God is asking us to settle, to plant, and to pray and work for the prosperity of the community. We are to turn evil into good. We are Kingdom people who refuse to be destroyed by evil. We transform any situation because we have hope. There is hope for a life before death because God is a God of promises and God keeps the promises given to us. God is the great dreamer and He can imagine the most wonderful things for us. He is creative and imaginative, and His ways are higher (better informed and original?) than my ways. There is a way forward, there is a way out of displacement.

We may be going through times of dryness in our spiritual life, times of desolation and despair (29:12-13). These experiences are normal, but they are just for a season. Our responsibility is to cultivate our relationship with Jesus, to pray, to study, and to serve. This is normal no matter if we feel God is close to us or not.

Faith gives us the inner certainty that there will be times of fruitfulness in our spiritual life again. There will be periods when God will come quickly as we pray. Suddenly there are divine appointments, where we meet the right people. There may be times when one thing after another just fall into place. We wonder why it is happening now, but God is saying that there are times when closeness to Jesus comes easily.

As we seek after Jesus with all our heart, we will find God (29:13-14). There are not many ways to God, there is only the Jesus Way. The wonderful thing is that the Jesus Way still has many facets and expressions and it may look Orthodox, Catholic, or Protestant.

As we continue to follow Jesus, we will experience a new start. A restoration will take place, as there is a way out of the wilderness. We may be back in similar situations and ministries like before, but we are different. We have been through the faith desert where all we could do was to trust that God knows what He is doing. Things may have looked bleak, boring, and unfair, but it has been a healing journey and a time of faith development. At that moment we know in our body and spirit that we are truly free at last. We are ready to face our past again, to be sent into situations that may have crushed us in previously. We have learnt to stand in Christ and have a better understanding of who we are in Christ. We have become stronger in spirit. *"Your Kingdom come, your will be done"* can now become our battle cry. Now we can minister healing, forgiveness, and reconciliation as we have become reconciled to ourselves and to God.

A False Start – A New Beginning

Luke 5:1-11 (David Bentley Hart Translation)

1 And it happened that, as the crowd pressed in upon him and listened to God's word, and as he stood by the Lake of Gennesaret,

2 He then saw two boats standing at the lake's edge; and the fishermen, having disembarked from them, were washing the nets.

3 And embarking in one of the boats, which belonged to Simon, he asked him to put out a little from the land; and sitting down he taught the crowds from the boat.

4 And when he ceased speaking he said to Simon, "Put out into the deep, and let your nets down for a haul."

5 And in reply Simon said, "Master, we laboured all through the night and took in nothing; but on your word I will let down the nets."

6 And when they did so they ensnared an immense multitude of fishes, and their nets were being torn.

7 And they signalled to their fellows in the other boat that they should come to help them; and they came, and they filled both boats, so much so that they were sinking.

8 And seeing this, Simon Peter fell at the knees of Jesus, saying, "Go from me, Lord, for I am a sinful man."

9 For amazement had seized him and all those with him at the haul of fishes that they gathered -

10 And so likewise both James and John, the sons of Zebedee, who were partners with Simon. And Jesus said to Simon, "Do not be afraid; from now on you will be capturing men."

11 And, bringing the boats back onto the land, they abandoned everything and followed him.

(This reflection might be a bit confusing because I have tried to imagine myself as Peter. What would I feel, think, and how might I react? I also bring my personal experiences to the reflection to see how the spirit of the passage may help me towards wholeness, integration, and salvation).

IT WAS A morning like any other but not quite. Jesus was surrounded by people as it had become commonplace (5:1). He knew how to draw a crowd and work a crowd. People were so captivated by His words and miracles that it was difficult to keep them away. We were so desperate as a people facing oppression, poverty, and a lack of opportunities.

Time and again, we heard of different people who had come to free us, but our hope grew cold quickly. They did not deliver, and the Romans were quick to kill off any signs of optimism. However, Jesus was different.

There were so many people around that they kept on shouting, "louder". They wanted to hang on to his every word, but it was difficult to pick up everything with all the hustle and bustle. We had already emptied the boats and were cleaning the fishing nets (5:2). Noticing the empty boats, Jesus got the idea to speak from one of them, so people could hear Him better.

We were minding our own business, but it was difficult not to eavesdrop on what Jesus was talking about. I enjoyed His teaching, but I have mouths to feed, so I cannot follow Him days on end. Some did, and I admire that. While cleaning the nets, I smiled as I was reminded of the time when Jesus said to Martha that she was too busy with all the hosting and paid too little attention to God's word (Luke 10:41). I could identify with Martha. It is good and fine to be a disciple, but how do you manage when you have family commitments and a small business to run? People were depending on me. Can I just follow Him and forget about them? I could not fathom how they were able to take such a step? How did they make ends meet when we earn so little already?

Jesus asked me if He could use my boat (5:3). Of course, no problem. We always lend stuff to each other and share in our small communities, otherwise we would never survive. You learn that when you are poor. Either you live in community caring for each other, or you go under.

He asked me to push the boat out, and then He got going. People looked on with great expectation and some sat down on the shore. Seeing their faces was something else. So much hope was written in their eyes. Maybe this was it? Maybe He was our Messianic Liberator?

I couldn't help it. I listened to most of the teaching while I was working on the fishing nets. It was nice. Sometimes I got lost in thought. Jesus's teaching made so much sense and His words made a home in my heart.

Suddenly, everything changed for me. I was pulled out of a dream-like state of contemplating a brighter future when Jesus called my name (5:4). I did not get it at first. Jesus wanted me to go fishing again! He gave some clear instructions; we had to sail out once more and wait until we reached the deep sea before casting our nets.

My tiredness hit me before I was fully able to make sense of His words (5:5). We had worked and worked. It had been an all-nighter and we had caught nothing. We were tired and fed up. We had done all the work for nothing.

I remember that feeling all too well from pioneering and leading a Christian ministry in the UK for 18 years. I had set up a charity to deliver social action projects in the local community as a ministry of the church I was pastoring. At the busiest time, we had 23 staff. We did many exciting things working with a diverse group of people in our community. Our staff team was (most of the time!) wonderful, and we had people from different backgrounds. It was fun but challenging.

At some point I was stuck between a rock and a hard place. I had done everything I could think of. I had worked stupid hours for many months. We had networked, researched, applied for money, organised new projects, done advertising, prayed, and fasted. You name it, we had done it. And the result: No money, no grants, no contracts! We had done a marvellous job in our projects. The users and students loved what we were offering, the government agencies gave us good grades at the inspections, and people praised our work. It made no difference. Political games and, I guess, spiritual battles finished off our work.

Some Christians said to me: "God is never late", "God will make a way", "God will provide." Sometimes I felt like screaming. If they were so sure about that, why then did no money come in, why did we not win the contracts like we used to? The encouraging words became Christian clichés to my ears as the staff and I lived with the workload and the insecurity. I felt the responsibility for my fellow staff, their families and our service users weighing on my shoulders. I often felt like the apostle Paul, who talked about caring and praying day and night for the churches (2 Corinthians 11:28). Leadership is a joy as well as a burden.

It was a tiring period. I may not have been cleaning nets, but we were emptying lofts, clearing out storage rooms, organising files, finishing the accounts, and dumping many things in a skip. Everything had to go in the end, and I had to say goodbye to friends and fellow staff members who had served the community, God, and our charity so well. It was devastating. There was so much pain.

I can empathise with Peter. I felt his exhaustion after doing a lot of work that led to absolutely nothing except redundancies, and some staff even had to leave the country. In the end, we had to close a wonderful ministry that was helping thousands of people every year.

In Galilee, we lived from hand to mouth. *"Give us this day our daily bread"* (Matthew 6:11, English Standard Version), was the cry of our hearts. Right now, I thought, why bother? We had worked, we were almost finished with the nets and I just wanted to sleep and try to schedule some worry time about my finances for another day.

What do you do when Jesus is the one asking you to do something? I did allow Him to use my boat. I pushed it out myself. Now, there was another request. I know He always worked hard, but did I have any strength left for hard physical work, and did I have the emotional resilience to cope with the possibility of another failure if I returned with no fish?

I decided to give it a go. Jesus was a mate, and Jesus did so much good for others and for me as well. He was full of surprises so maybe He had something up His sleeve?

I agreed to give it a go - reluctantly. This time it was a revelation straight from the Lord. It was not just one of somebody's favourite inspirational quotes from the Bible. Sometimes we need to own the revelation ourselves, allowing the words of others to be a confirmation, and nothing but a confirmation.

Back at the lake, we threw out the nets and something happened. The nets filled up and our nets could not cope with the overwhelming catch (5:6). From being empty handed, depressed, and tired people, we came to be excited, motivated, and joyful men. In an instant our perspective changed. We changed. We saw God in action. We saw that God cared about the things we cared for. We needed a catch to live. We were experienced, but our experience, our years of hard labour and of refining our skills had not given the results we needed. We got a glimpse of God's Kingdom and how the Kingdom works. It was staggering and overwhelming.

I called my brothers for help (5:7). They too were blessed in the process. I think they felt they were too blessed, because their boat became extremely heavy under the weight of all the fish. It was unbelievable. I know that God does things for other people; but experiencing His grace in such a practical and dramatic way was astonishing.

I my personal life, I have wondered how to respond to grace when it hits me? I felt unworthy. I knew that I did not deserve the love of God (5:8). I felt sinful. I knew that I had tried to protect myself and my family by hiding and trying to be what people wanted me to be. I had fasted for 40 days a couple of times. I had worked among the poor. I had given away more than 10% of my income to the church and to God's work. I had tried to be good, holy, and acceptable in God's sight, but I had ended up empty handed anyway. Often, I felt that I deserved God's blessing and breakthroughs, because my family and I had really tried to do His will through our churches and ministries. Trying to be a good disciple and a pastor for many years had left me disappointed with God. He did not help me to save our charity! He did not save the jobs, so what is the point of doing all this good work and my commitment to spiritual disciplines? What good is it trying to live a straight life when it leads to pain and personal suffering? I just had to give up and give in.

Later God bestowed His grace upon me. I was unsure how to contain it and respond to it.

When coming out, God told me that most opportunities for ministry would be closed to me, but that He would open the doors.

My experience merged with that of Peter. Now, I knew deep within that I did not earn God's grace. Now, I knew that no matter how much I prayed or fasted; the evangelical church would not be waiting for me with open arms. Ministry opportunities would have to be a God thing.

Later, I experienced God in action; an article was written about me in the Christian newspaper and another one in the LGBT magazine, a podcast interview, an invitation to preach, a part-time job, an interview for a chapter in a book, an invitation to teach, etc. I have preached on grace and love many times, but God gave me some incredibly deep one-to-one lessons. I knew I did not deserve these openings.

I noticed how ungrateful I have been in the past. How much I have tried to gain God's attention and love by certain behaviours. The things in themselves were not wrong, but my motivation was wrong, which influenced my view of God and my relationship with God. I had become the older grumpy brother in the story of the prodigal son (Luke 15:11-32). I believed that I deserved God's blessing and help, and I was angry and confused because God did not act the way I felt He should.

I came to realise some of my shortcomings but also the harsh reality of the Christian world: Many see me as toxic because of being gay and the fruit of my life has become irrelevant. This is a hard pill to swallow, but on the other hand, it makes me see the glory of God, the love of God, and the grace of God in a new way. Now, I can truly say that any ministry opportunity is because of grace as I can do nothing to impress the Christian (evangelical) world.

I am not the only one being amazed (5:9). When we share our blessings with others, they see God too. They notice His work in my life and in their lives through me. People read our lives, also when we are despairing. They read if we compromise or if we live with integrity. They notice if we turn to God or try to make our own way. They notice anger and bitterness or gratitude and love.

I want my life continually to be transformed by the light and the beauty of our Lord. Because of His grace, I can approach Him without being so angry and annoying.

I am learning about obedience too. It is a difficult word for my Western mindset. Obedience sounds like somebody submitting themselves to abuse as they turn off their discernment. Going out to sea again was an act of obedience and surrender for Peter. It was an act of faith.

I think of the song we sing in church, "I surrender all." I have wondered what it means practically. To me it means to listen to the heart of Jesus and to follow Him. Love and faith in action. It is simple, yet profound.

It was inconvenient for Peter to go fishing again, but he followed Jesus's advice. There was a risk, but in this situation the risk paid off. After this wonderful blessing Jesus told Peter not to fear his new ministry (5:10). The fishing was for a time, but it was a "false start." They were in training for their real assignment.

Maybe I lost my community ministry in the UK, so I would be available for the next phase in life and ministry? Maybe it was not such a bad thing, even though it hurt so much at the time. I felt that I had failed people no matter how many hours I had put in daily. I felt that my responsibility was for the ministry to continue, but I am learning, that I cannot hold tightly to the ministry of God. It is His ministry, not mine. I am the caretaker of His work for as long as He wants it. I might face opposition and the Devil may get the upper hand at times, but ultimately, God will win. Our lives are in His hands and even if we lose our lives, then nothing can separate us from the love of God. I knew that, but my spirit and emotions do not always get it. I want things to be different. I want to get justice now. I want the ministry to be successful and recognised. I want to be recognised and valued!

I am learning that I must give up on my need for status and success. Sometimes even at the best of times, we lose. We may have worked hard, but things may fall apart anyway: A relationship, a job, an education, our finances, the ministry, etc. Sometimes life is just unfair, but Jesus wants to pick us up and send us out to fish again, so He can get our attention. He pushes us out of our comfort zones, but also out of our self-pity. At that moment He can redirect us, when we are all ears.

Maybe I am readier now to let go of everything that holds me back: The need for success and prestige and the need to look spiritual in the eyes of my fellow Christians. God reached me when I was sulking after I closed our wonderful community ministry. I had given 18 years of my life to this ministry together with my family. Letting go of it tore me apart, but God is healing my hurting heart. Now, I am noticing that there is a future. I see in the spirit a new ministry emerging. A new day is dawning. I am not sure how it will come about, but hope is growing within me and maybe Jesus is also saying to you and me, "do not fear the next chapter in your life."

Enjoy the Imperfect Now

Psalm 23 (The Passion Translation)

1 The Lord is my Best Friend and my Shepherd. I always have more than enough.

2 He offers a resting place for me in his luxurious love. His tracks take me to an oasis of peace, the quiet brook of bliss.

3 That's where he restores and revives my life. He opens before me pathways to God's pleasure, and leads me along in his footsteps of righteousness so that I can bring honour to his name

4 Lord, even when your path takes me through the valley of deepest darkness, fear will never conquer me, for you already have! You remain close to me and lead me through it all the way. Your authority is my strength and my peace. The comfort of your love takes away my fear. I'll never be lonely, for you are near.

5 You become my delicious feast even when my enemies dare to fight. You anoint me with the fragrance of your Holy Spirit, you give me all I can drink of you until my heart overflows.

6 So why would I fear the future? I'm being pursued only by your goodness and unfailing love. Then afterwards – when my life is through, I'll return to your glorious presence to be forever with you!

SOMETIMES MY EMOTIONS tell me that the Bible is probably not true. It is sort of true, but I cannot depend on it and believe the promises. Those promises are either too grand or not meant for me. Even if they were meant for me, I would probably lose out because of the spiritual battle that I face: Just like in any war, there are casualties of war and I will always be one of them! I am not always an optimist!

I realise that I do not always have the most positive view of God or myself. In the past it was not uncommon for me to tell people that God was grumpy on the day he created me, so I was like a car made of faulty bits. I am the odd one out. But Psalm 23 always challenges my emotional responses. Maybe there is more to life than what I expect? Maybe a loving God will engage much more with me that I dare to hope for?

David wrote this beautiful psalm possibly when he was just a teenage boy. Maybe he did not really know the challenges of the world, e.g. the poverty of most of his fellow Israelites? Maybe he was just a bit naive or maybe he had learnt to trust God the hard way?

David sees God as a great shepherd (23:1). The kind of shepherd you can rely on. The one who is always there when needed. It is almost like capturing the mind of a child. Children trust unconditionally in their parents and their parents' abilities. They have not been corrupted by disappointments and by comparing their upbringing to that of others. They just trust that their parents are there for them when they need it.

As children grow up, they realise that parents are not able to do all that is needed, and even their own parents do not have superpowers to repair all things or heal all things.

How different things are with God, and David captured that. God is dependable, and David concluded that he had more than enough. He had what he needed for now. It is an incredible statement and the kind of statement that challenges me. I often feel that I lack something. I lack money, friendships, a husband, the right ministry, a holiday, and all the other things on my heart. Some of the things are very real needs and other things are dreams and longings, but emotionally, I really, really need these things – now!

When people ask me how I am doing, I might answer very well, but then add some of the things that are still a challenge to me. I easily focus on what I need instead of what I have. I see the need so much clearer and miss the gratitude for all the things that God has done. Maybe I am quite an ungrateful kind of guy, but David had trained his heart to appreciate God right here, right now.

David was able to enjoy the imperfect now. He could see the goodness of God, even when he was alone in the fields watching the sheep. He could trust God to provide for the days ahead even though he knew hunger. Maybe the key is contentment. As Paul wrote, *"I know what it is to be in need, and I know what it is to have plenty. I have learned the secret of being content in any and every situation, whether well fed or hungry, whether living in plenty or in want"* (Philippians 4:12, New International Version).

David was not lying, when he said that he had more than enough. He had learnt to be content and to trust God for his life. That does not mean that everything would go according to plan, but he believed that he was in God's hands.

It reminds me of a saying of Ignatius of Loyola (1491 - 1556): "As far as we are concerned, we should not prefer health to sickness, riches to poverty, honour to dishonour, a long life to a short life. The same holds for all other things."

A quote like that is so hard for me to understand and appreciate. It takes a lot of reflection for me to come to terms with it and maybe even embrace it. Can I truly pray that it is ok for me to live a shorter life, when my desire is to live a long and healthy life full of meaningful moments?

David held the moment. He did not need to have all the answers. He coped with uncertainty, because he trusted in God's love.

As a gay man I have so often longed for God's protection. That God would soothe me when people's words and actions cut deep into my soul with discouragement. Some of my close allies were not trustworthy in a moment of vulnerability. So, I learnt that people cannot always be trusted, and I have in some ways projected that unto God. How unfair is that? I will never learn to be content in God and to sense that I have more than enough, if I hold on to a negative image.

The false spirit is wrapping me around his finger like he did with Eve. Adam and Eve had practically everything. They had direct access to God. They had a whole garden of opportunities. God was not a no-saying God. He was all "Yes" to them. There was only one thing they could not do. Only one thing was off limit. We have turned it the other way around as if God says no to everything and there are only a few good things available to humankind. As a result, we Christians have become boring, guilt-ridden and spoilsports. This is so opposite to the reality of God, but the false spirit succeeds in twisting our thinking (Genesis 3:1-7). Lord, renew my mind, so I may see what David saw. Help me to believe that "I always have more than enough" even when I feel I am running on empty.

Maybe part of this renewal is to let God do His work in us. But for him to do that, we need to learn to retreat from all the demands from ourselves, the world and the spiritual and cultural climate.

We can find our rest in God (23:2). I sense that there is such a difference in how I react depending on who I am with. With certain people I feel that I must weigh every word before I speak. I need to ensure that everything is perfect, because otherwise they will call me out. In those situations, I become tense, and I try to protect myself. I become defensive and stressed.

For many years, I saw God as somebody deeply disappointed in me. No matter what I did the pray the gay away, it was just not enough. The books told me that it was because I did not try hard enough, I was not fully invested in getting healed. It is amazing how we as Christians sometimes place burdens on each other in our eagerness to stand out as holy and committed to the full Gospel: *"They crush people with unbearable religious demands and never lift a finger to ease the burden"* (Matthew 23:4, The Living Bible Translation).

God is not displeased with us. He is the lover of our souls. He is the one who draws us into His love, His loving embrace. Without it, how can we find rest in this world? LGBT+ Christians understand, more than many, the concept of being "aliens" to this world. We are always in the minority no matter where we go. We must scan the environment and consider our words and actions.

This wonderful God wants to take us to a resting place in his love. He wants to create pathways for us to experience His pleasure and peace (23:2). He is the Way, but at times we may reject that way, because we have been so hurt by the teachings of the church. Sometimes LGBT+ Christians are caught between two unfriendly groups. Some churches do not believe you can be Christian and LGBT+, and at the same time there are LGBT+ communities that are so angry with the church, that they do not want to welcome LGBT+ Christians. We are perceived as enemies by some Christians and by some LGBT+ groups. That is a very real tension for many. We so need time with God to heal. We need His peace that surpasses all understanding to be able to stand. We need to retreat to His love.

I feel challenged to find time to hear His voice of love, to wait upon the Lord, so He can renew my strength. I want to move on, but sometimes I am just exhausted, drained, and tired. So, LGBT+ family, let's find God in the quiet. Let Him speak to us about His love, so we find freedom and healing from traumatic experiences. Let Him convince us deep in our spirits that we are loved by Him and we do not need to reject all church communities, the Bible, and the fellowship of the saints. We are God's children even if the church thinks differently.

I am learning from the Quaker tradition to wait expectantly upon the Holy Spirit. Being alone, I typically sit in the quiet for 60 minutes. To begin with I settle down to the silence by letting go and naming all the things on top of my head. It may be things of the past or things of the future. I notice them and let them go. Then I ask God to speak into the silence. I notice my breath, and what it does to my body. I try not to pray or to meditate, because then I am still using words. The purpose for this time of silent worship is to still my own voice and thoughts to let God say or do what He wants to do. Then I wait and listen with all my senses. I get the impression that healing is taking place during these sessions even when I do not know what is going on. I often have a few impressions by the end of the 60 minutes that I write down in my spiritual journal. I try to let the solutions come to me in the quiet.

Jesus is not only our destination, He is our journey, our pathway, our way to life. In His love we are being restored and revived (23:3), but it takes time. I need to learn to slow down enough to catch my breath. Do I dare to surrender my life right here, right now even if I do not know where it will take me? Do I trust that God has a future for me and wants the best for me, or will I compromise like Eve because I have come to believe that God keeps the best from me?

Notice how He opens pathways to God's pleasure and fairness (23:3). I do not know how you connect with God and learn from Him, but there are different pathways. He may renew you through prayer or Bible meditation. He may soothe you through gospel music or classical music, or when you go for a walk in nature. He may give you hope through reading Christian books or attending a Bible study.

We may not experience fairness all the time, but He is fair and just. When I walk in His ways, then I am blessing others with fairness. I can give, what I have not yet received myself, because Jesus is the giver of life. In my own life, I have often felt unprotected, and I have noticed how that has created a default position in my adult life to try to protect my family, the church, or my staff. I want them to experience a life different to mine when it comes to feeling emotionally protected and safe. Saying that, I am beginning to experience God's care in new ways. His touch, His kiss, His kindness. I am seeing a bigger picture, getting a bigger revelation of the Jesus that I love and serve.

Jesus is our breakthrough. He has gone before us, and therefore he can take me down pathways I have not walked before. He draws, pulls, and urges me to be on the move. He wants me to move closer to His heart and to understand Him so truth can set me free. Truth is not an insight; it is a person. Jesus is the truth that sets us free. There is abundant life available, instead of the drained reality that many of us face daily (John 10:10).

Psalm 23 started so well, and then something spoilt the mood. Sometimes life is just a very dark place (23:4). I do not like the darkness, I never have. I did not like the darkness or being at home alone as I grew up. I have also noticed that some of my LGBT+ friends feel uncomfortable about nights alone.

The darkness can give us the feeling of a life out of control. Something is going on, but we do not know what it is. We try to perceive what is happening to us, but there is no clarity.

Darkness can be a place of restoration, though. Our first experience was the safety of the womb, the dark home of our mothers. The Jewish day starts at sunset, so we start the day by getting rest and feeling safe in the hands of God. We let go and let darkness envelope us and revive us. It is when we sleep that our bodies heal, and our dreams help us become whole.

The dark periods of our lives may not be an enemy, but a time to learn to trust God; to trust that His rod and His staff will comfort me, even when I do not see what He is doing.

I remember a time while leading a church movement when I found it hard to get any guidance from God about my personal life or the church movement. I felt so bad about it as it went on for quite some time. I became insecure about some strategic decisions; I wanted to do God's will, but I felt I did not know what God wanted in this specific situation.

I left for India to be with some of our pastors and leaders and I realised that it was not just me. Collectively, we were in the dark, and together we had to find ways to trust that God was at work even when we could not see what He was up to. It was a time to grow in our spiritual lives together, learning to trust and not fear decision making and the future. God was with us even when we did not have any clear guidance. David encouraged us to believe in God's authority. He is the same no matter what I feel or experience, He is with me no matter if it is day or night, or if I am in a period of clarity or fighting in the dark.

Darkness can also feel like loneliness. There are times when we do not even notice when people care, or when they reach out to us. Our minds are so full of insecurity or fear that we miss the comfort of God and people. How do we respond to darker sides and periods of our lives? Do we let the darkness rebuild us or will it become a source of detachment from God and other people? God reminded me that I may feel lonely, but I am never alone. Immanuel, the God who is with us, is asking us to take refuge, residence in Him always.

David knew fighting all too well. He was used to wild animals waiting for the right moment to attack the most vulnerable of the flock. He had learnt to deal with the lion and the bear, the dangers of his life. Sometimes the LGBT+ communities become the centre of the spiritual battles in society. We are accused of all evil, the breakdown of the family, tornadoes, viruses, and natural disasters. We are told that we must stay single if we want a comfortable afterlife. Sometimes the voices and the actions are incredibly forceful and damaging. Politicians and Christians fight against the "gay onslaught" with great zeal in many places.

David takes us back to the love of God and the infilling of the Holy Spirit (23:5). That is our true home no matter what happens around us. Nobody can take away the work of the Holy Spirit in our lives, and we can drink until our hearts overflow. We need deep healing and a healing that overflows to the rest of society. God is turning our painful experiences around for good as we become healers of communities in the power of the Holy Spirit. I want to attempt to follow this wonderful life changing way of living, the Kingdom way, that Jesus talked about: *"I'm telling you to love your enemies. Let them bring out the best in you, not the worst. When someone gives you a hard time, respond with the energies of prayer, for then you are working out of your true selves, your God-created selves"* (Matthew 5:44-45, The Message Translation)

I am beginning to understand why I need to retreat, to find God's path, to be revived and restored. If not, then the hurtful situations just stick with me and I harden my heart and become like my opponents. I lose the Kingdom and I lose the heart of God. I become ugly in my

172 REV. DR. ARNO STEEN ANDREASEN

fight for fairness instead of trusting that God will help me to heal and to make things right. There is something people need to see in me to change their views and their actions. They need to see the Holy Spirit in my life. They need to see that God has not abandoned me or us, and maybe that will be a greater revelation than all the theological arguments in the world.

Will I get the future that I am hoping for? Will we see a just society for the LGBT+ communities and many other minority groups? I do not know how far we will get, but David told me not to fear the future (23:6). Politicians come and go; pastors come and go. There are seasons of blessing and seasons of hardship. We live, and we die. There are times when I feel like I am being pursued by challenges and I am desperate for breakthrough. But David is helping me to see a parallel reality. I am also being pursued by goodness and unfailing love. I think I can live with that.

A Rare Breed

Ephesians 2:11-22 (The Passion Translation)

11-12 So don't forget that you were not born as Jews and were uncircumcised (circumcision itself is just a work of man's hands); you had none of the Jewish covenants and laws; you were foreigners to Israel's incredible heritage; you were without the covenants and prophetic promises of the Messiah, the promised hope, and without God.

13 Yet look at you now! Everything is new! Although you were once distant and far away from God, now you have been brought delightfully close to him through the sacred blood of Jesus - you have actually been united to Christ!

14 Our reconciling "Peace" is Jesus! He has made Jew and non-Jew one in Christ. By dying as our sacrifice, he has broken down every wall of prejudice that separated us and has now made us equal through our union with Christ.

15 Ethnic hatred has been dissolved by the crucifixion of his precious body on the cross. The legal code that stood condemning every one of us has now been repealed by his command. His triune essence has made peace between us by starting over - forming one new race of humanity, Jews and non-Jews fused together!

16 Two have now become one, and we live restored to God and reconciled in the body of Christ. Through his crucifixion, hatred died.

¹⁷ For the Messiah has come to preach this sweet message of peace to you, the ones who were distant, and to those who are near.

¹⁸ And now, because we are united to Christ, we both have equal and direct access in the realm of the Holy Spirit to come before the Father!

¹⁹ So, you are not foreigners or guests, but rather you are the children of the city of the holy ones, with all the rights as family members of the household of God.

²⁰ You are rising like the perfectly fitted stones of the temple; and your lives are being built up together upon the ideal foundation laid by the apostles and prophets, and best of all, you are connected to the Head Cornerstone of the building, the Anointed One, Jesus Christ himself!

²¹ This entire building is under construction and is continually growing under his supervision until it rises up completed as the holy temple of the Lord himself.

²² This means that God is transforming each one of you into the Holy of Holies, his dwelling place, through the power of the Holy Spirit living in you!

SOME YEARS AGO, when I was applying for a job, I was called into a meeting with the consultant at the agency. We discussed the position and my background. After some time, the consultant concluded, that I "was a rare breed." He explained that I had an unusual combination of theoretical knowledge and practical experience at different levels. He said that getting a job would probably be tough for me, as it would be difficult to find a place where I would fit in. On the other hand, when I found the place, it would be a perfect fit.

I do not know if that was supposed to be encouraging or not, but I think there is something to it. I am not easily contented, and I often feel like an outsider. I guess many of us feel like that especially when we are part of a minority group. Being gay means that I will always be in a minority position. I cannot exactly recruit people to become gay, even though some people think we can influence the minds of vulnerable people, so they suddenly catch the deceptive gay virus.

Paul is writing to the Ephesians about the racial divisions between Jews and non-Jews or gentiles (2:11-12). At a time of waves of asylum seekers and refugees, the debate about culture, religion and race has become a political hot potato - again. In some ways, it never really left the church either. Try to discuss Israel and Palestine and you know that the issue of race is still extremely important to us. Christians have not become one as Paul proclaimed in his letter. We are still divided into many different groups, and how we love categorising: male/female, straight/LGBT, white or black, educated or working class, Muslim or Christian, religious or secular and the list goes on. We keep on defining ourselves as part of a tribe and wanting to protect this tribe even if it is not in any danger.

As a gay man I know what it means to be an alien, a stranger, or a foreigner in this world and especially when it comes to church. Maybe that is one of the gifts of the LGBT+ communities to the church. We know what it is like to be standing outside looking in. We know what it is like sitting in the pew as a closeted LGBT+ person listening to people preaching that you cannot be Christian and gay. People talk about us as if we were not there, but we take it all in year in and year out. We pretend to be part of the community, but we know that people may only like the image that we present. They may not like the full story about our lives. We just sit there with worry in our hearts. It has become popular to say that the church is inclusive to all, but what they really mean is that they have become welcoming. They still do not have the theology nor the statutes to be truly inclusive and affirming. They still put up glass ceilings for

LGBT+ Christians; there are limits to what we may do, say, and the positions we may hold in the church.

I remember being at a prophetic meeting as a new Christian. I ended up against the wall at the back of the hall, praying all the way through the meeting for forgiveness for being gay, as I was so scared of being called to the front and having my gayness proclaimed to all. The environment that should have enriched and helped me into the arms of my loving Saviour scared me because of the teaching that I had heard in the church. That is not love, that is fear, and fear does not come from the God who says, "Do not fear."

We need to reclaim our salvation as part of one people group, the new breed of God (2:13). We will never be free until we have a revelation of God's love that covers a multitude of sins, also my sins. We will never find peace with God if we are afraid of God. We will never live in the power of the Holy Spirit if we see ourselves as the gentiles who are not good enough for God. I am saved by grace just like anybody else. There is nothing else that can save me, not even celibacy. It is through Jesus that I am united to God, so why am I still hurt every time I hear a Christian tell me that I am condemned to the eternal fire? I need to grasp the truth of God's word for myself, so the truth can set me free. I need to trust what the Spirit is saying to all of us who follow Jesus, that "… *if anyone is in Christ, the new creation has come: The old has gone, the new is here!*" (2 Corinthians 5:18, New International Version). I cannot do anything to earn my salvation, nor avoid doing something (by not having sex) to stay saved.

For decades, the debate about LGBT+ inclusion in the church has been so unequal. In my opinion, the theological debate and testimonies in the evangelical wing of the church have been quite one-sided. From my experience, if an LGBT+ person is asked to share a testimony in the church, then the person will stand up and say that the person is now living a straight lifestyle. That is the true sign of victory over the evil of being gay, so that is a real testimony and we all cheer. But what about a testimony from an LGBT+ couple who have stayed together for decades serving God? That picture does not fit the politics of the church, so that is not allowed. After all, you cannot really follow God if you are in a relationship as an LGBT+ person! We learn that we are enemies of God.

If Jesus is our Peace, then maybe it is not just Jew and gentile who are one in Christ (2:14). Maybe it is also male and female, slave and free as well as LGBT+ and straight. The terms of salvation are, after all, the same. Everything that separated us from salvation is gone if we believe in the saving power of Jesus. He overwrites our theological arguments, and His Spirit is present in the lives of those who follow Him. Can you imagine what would happen if we truly believed that "*he has broken down every wall of prejudice that separated us and has now made us equal through our union with Christ*" (2:14)?

There are no special categories for LGBT+ people, but sometimes it feels like there are: You can be saved if you live like a straight person, even if you are attracted to somebody of your own gender. You can be saved if you do not have sex. You can be saved if you renounce being gay. You can be saved if you.... All these demands are not in the Bible, they are based on our tradition. Instead, the walls have come down in Christ. We are all saved the same way. There are no extra demands on people who are LGBT+. Our calling is to follow Him wherever that takes us. We are united through following and loving Christ and all His children. It is time for the church to celebrate the unity we have in Christ, so the world will see that we are truly His disciples because we love one another.

Paul stated that "*ethnic hatred has been dissolved by the crucifixion*" and so has any other man-made divisions (2:15). We are good at creating superiority groups in the different cultures, but Paul said it is time to lay aside everything that divides us. The church of Christ came together at the cross of Jesus. We were fused together, and nothing shall be allowed to divide us. When we allow that to happen, then confusion, evil, and division win the day. Doors are opened for oppression just like in New Testament times when Jewish congregations felt that they were the true followers of Christ and that the gentile believers had to become circumcised like them to fit in.

I am not called to be like a straight man. I am called to be like Christ. That is the pilgrimage we all need to make. We journey toward Christ as we worship and follow Him. It is interesting to read Paul's words. He wrote, "*The legal code that stood condemning every one of us has been repealed by his command*" (2:15). The Old Testament and especially Leviticus has often been used against the LGBT+ communities, but Paul stated, that the legal framework of the Old Testament condemned us all. Now it is time to break free of that because it has been repealed by God on the cross. There is no condemnation for LGBT+ believers any longer. Instead, all believers no matter our background and status have been merged into a new God-people, a new breed, a new humanity. Now, it is time to behave like new humans because we are clothed in Christ.

All the laws of the Old Testament have been fulfilled in Christ. The laws could not save, they could only condemn, but Jesus came to save. That is why we learn that the Great Commandment sums up the Old Testament. We are here to love Christ and love our neighbour. Nothing more, nothing less, which is a lifelong task and challenge.

In the Bible there are only two racial groups. There are the Jews and the non-Jews. The non-Jews consisted of all kinds of ethnic groups, but that was irrelevant. Either they were born into the Jewish race or not. The Jewish race was called to love God and to show the world how to live with God and have God as their King. They should not have their own king like their neighbours as they were called to be different. They were to learn to depend on God for their lives. He sent them manna, He provided water in the desert, and He protected them from their enemies. God was to be the foundation and the very fabric of their society. No matter if they succeeded or not, they still had the calling to live close to God, trusting Him. Therefore, Paul was only talking about reconciling two groups: gentiles and Jews, and that means that we are all included.

We notice that in God's salvation plan, the two people groups have become one (2:16). We are restored to God. In the same way, God is asking us to break down every barrier that stops us from being one. We may not agree about everything, but we are one Body of Christ. It is amazing to read that hatred died at the cross, when we face so much homophobia, biphobia, and transphobia also from the church. The language used by some of the Christian celebrities could sound like hatred to my ears, even though they tell us it comes from a loving heart. The argument goes something like this: Like an unruly child, the LGBT+ communities must be disciplined and truth hurts! Well, in Christ hatred died. In Christ we are restored to God and reconciled in His Body. I am in His Body even when others say I am not. They can throw me out of the church, but they cannot throw me out of the mystical Body of Christ. He is the Head of His Body and I am so grateful for that.

Sometimes I get so upset. Minority stress is a very real thing. I need Jesus to speak peace to me, so I do not distance myself from His love out of fear (2:17). I had to start on a new journey to get to know the Christ of the Bible. I found that there were so many things I assumed about Jesus, that I did not even notice when the Bible said something different. I am learning to come back to His message of shalom and allowing Him to reveal life transforming wholeness to my heart and mind. I am no longer distant in my worship and jealous of the way God is using and blessing my friends. Now, I know His loving grace and how He can use me when I allow Him to use all of me, the authentic, integrated me. My friends and I have equal access to His Holy Spirit (2:18). I am not placed outside His grace or His ability to reach me. It is not more difficult for me to come before the Creator God compared to anybody else. *"The Kingdom of Heaven is at hand"* (Matthew 3:2) so we can all grab hold of it.

As LGBT+ Christians, we are part of the household of God (2:19). We have the same rights as anybody else and we are the holy ones as well, no matter what people tell us. I need to hold on to the liberating words of the Bible instead of the words of Christians with a classic interpretation of the Bible. I am not an alien in the house of God. I am a member. I do not have to feel like an outsider anymore. I am not a guest whose only role is to sit in the pew and pay my tithes. I am part of the priesthood of all believers and I am here to serve. I am to serve my God and minister to the world with love. This is life transforming. It is my role to be creative and to find ways to serve. It is my responsibility to find a church where there are no divisions among believers. My life fits perfectly into the Body of Christ (2:20). God has fitted us together for a purpose. Every stone, every person has a role to play. Do I hear an amen?

It is exciting to think about the way we fit together. Christ is at the centre of our faith and we follow in the footsteps of the apostolic and prophetic tradition (2:20). We have a history of unity, of oneness in Christ. When we work together, then the church is advancing and blessing people's lives. When we work together, then our mission becomes relevant to many people who are oppressed. Just think of the work of the church fighting for debt relief for the nations going under because of debt, or our help to people suffering due to human trafficking. The church is establishing schools, health clinics and rehabs that are lighthouses of a loving God to the nations. The prophets showed us how to stand against injustice, and the apostles showed us how to bring salvation to families and regions. Together we can focus on these tasks again instead of splitting churches and having endless debates about LGBT+ inclusion. We lost our way, but Jesus fitted us together, so why are we so eager to push people out?

We are under construction all the time as we have become the temple of the Holy Spirit (2:21-22). God is reconstructing our humanity through His Spirit as He transforms us through and through. As we follow Him, the fruit of the Spirit is developing in our lives. As we worship, we get a new understanding of the power of God at work in us and in the lives of fellow believers. Lord, help us to see that we are one race. Let us notice what God is doing, recognising that God is our Saviour, and we are not the Lord over the Body of Christ. How powerful it would be, if we stopped arguing against different Christian denominations, against women in ministry, against LGBT+ inclusion, against certain ethnic groups, against certain casts or tribes, against the poor. Imagine if we committed ourselves to seeing fellow Christians as our brothers and sisters. Imagine if we believed what Paul wrote in this letter: that the divisions are gone and there is only one way forward because we are a new race, a new humanity. I sense that miracles would happen, and we would all get a greater revelation of Christ.

Martin Luther King said something like this, "white supremacy is wrong, but black supremacy is just as wrong." In the Spirit of Paul and Dr. King, there is no longer Orthodox, Catholic and Protestant. There are no longer gender wars or ethnic hatred. There are no longer supremacy groups in the church, because believers are one in Christ and we love and accept that different groups worship and serve in different ways. Together, we become a beautiful mosaic, a picture of Christ's love to the world.

I Met an Angel

1 Kings 19:1-16 (The Orthodox Study Bible)

Now Ahab told Jezebel his wife everything Elijah did, and how he put to death the prophets with the sword.

2 Then Jezebel sent to Elijah, saying, "If you are Elijah and I this Jezebel, may God do so to me and more also if at this hour tomorrow, I do not make your life like the life of one of them."

3 Elijah was fearful, and he arose and ran for his life. He came to Beersheba of Judah, where he left his servant

4 But Elijah himself went a day's journey into the wilderness, and came and sat under a juniper tree. He prayed concerning his life, that he might die, and said, "I pray it be enough, O Lord. Now take my life, for I am no better than my fathers."

5 Then he lay down and slept under a tree. Unexpectedly, someone touched him and said to him, "Arise and eat."

6 Then Elijah looked, and there by his head was a cake made of wheat and a jar of water. So he ate and drank, and lay down again.

7 Again the angel of the Lord came back a second time, touched him and said, "Arise and eat, because the journey is great many days for you."

8 So he arose, ate and drank; and he went with the strength of that food forty days and forty nights, as far as Mount Horeb.

9 Here he went into a cave and rested. Behold, the word of the Lord came to him and said to him, "Elijah, what are you doing here?"

10 And Elijah said, "I have been very zealous for the Lord Almighty since the children of Israel have forsaken You. They tore down Your alters and killed Your prophets with the sword. I alone am left, and they seek to take my life."

11 Then He replied, "Go out tomorrow and stand on the mountain before the Lord; and behold, the Lord will pass by, and before the Lord, a great and powerful wind will be rending the mountains and shattering the rocks; but the Lord will not be in the wind. After the wind, an earthquake, but the Lord will not be in the earthquake.

12 After the earthquake, there will be a fire, but the Lord, will not be in the fire. After the fire, there will be a sound of a gentle breeze, and the Lord will be there."

13 So when Elijah heard this, he wrapped his face in his mantle, and went out and stood in the entrance of the cave. Suddenly a voice came to him and said, "Elijah, what are you doing here?"

14 He replied, I have been very zealous for the Lord Almighty, since the children of Israel have forsaken Your covenant, torn down Your alters, and killed Your prophets with the sword. I alone am left, and they seek to take my life."

15 Then the Lord said to him, "Go and return to your way to the desert of Damascus. When you arrive anoint Hazael as king over Syria.

16 You shall also anoint Jehu the son of Numshi as king over Israel, and shall anoint Elisah the son of Shaphat of Abel Meholah as prophet in your place."

I HAVE BEEN IN pioneering ministry for 18 years. I was a missionary to the UK and I also did some work in South Asia. It has been exciting and exhausting. In many ways, it was what I dreamt of before coming to Christ. A life that transformed lives, and where I had the opportunity to work with people around the world. But I was exhausted. There had been so many battles. Some were personal, and some were because of the ministry. The churches and our community projects were always in need of money. On top of that, we had all the different government inspections and they were a drain. The paperwork that we had to provide throughout the year, all the consultations, all the statistics, all the training, and all the politically correct terms we had to identify and use. There was so much pseudo-work, things we had to do that were irrelevant and pointless.

We had some great wins and we had a super staff team. In many ways, I was a blessed man. During some periods we were the flavour of the month, but with a change of government and "the winner takes it all" kind of political system in the UK, you can quickly fall from grace. I dared to speak out against the councillors and their decisions and ask questions about poverty and financial exploitation to the local MP (Member of Parliament). If you are clever, you do not do that, because then you get your butt whipped. Promises were made, but they did not deliver, and we still had salaries to pay!

I became cynical. I could not cope with more of the same. I did not trust our contract managers, councillors, and others in power anymore. Words had become cheap and they did not mean anything. I was searching for the person of peace, a person of integrity, but it looked like they had vanished into thin air. Whom to trust? What to do? I was falling apart due to anger and disappointment. It was not fair. I begged God, we prayed, we consulted, but to no avail. We were losing ground and important ministries. We had to lay off staff. Good people who had served this community for years. In general, they loved God and they loved the people we were serving.

As one councillor said to me, "You are dangerous because you influence a lot of people. You are a skilled networker and people listen to you." The result: they chose not to work with me and support our ministries.

I felt a bit like Elijah. He had been trying to do the right thing: To stop evil and to honour God in the process (19:1). He had been effective in ministry, but he had his battle wounds, because standing in the gap is exhausting. Now, he was told that the First Lady of the country wanted his head on a platter (19:2). She threatened him and his life's work.

How well we know this one in the LGBT+ communities. Personally, I have had people who believed they had the right to go through my private emails. All human rights and dignity went out of the window. I became fearful of them as well as angry. I guess that many of us are aware of people who have the power to destroy us, our reputations, and our relationships. I lived in fear of these people for years. And fear is crippling. We cannot think straight, and it is all too easy to make bad, stress-based decisions.

Elijah became fearful. He had been outed by the king and now he had the First Lady at his heels (19:3). He ran. How often is it that we end up running away, because we do not have the energy, the emotional safety net, or people to fight our corner? Like Elijah, we often face some very lonely battles. So, Elijah ran. It looked like a typical fight or flight response, and he chose flight. Get out of the situation and hide, quick.

We are so used to the closet, but some of us hate the closet. Hate having to watch our words, our mannerisms, and our conversation topics. Can I tell fellow Christians that I attended several talks at the Pride week, can I say that I went to the cinema and loved the latest

LGBT+ film? It does not take much for me to be accused of parading my sexuality, when I am just talking about watching a film, listening to an artist or attending a lecture. So, we run back into the closet and we sulk, like Elijah, but more about that later.

Elijah went into the wilderness to gather his thoughts (19:4). He had parked his servant in Beersheba, maybe to protect him from harm or because he was so overstimulated by fear that he wanted to isolate himself from the world.

He prayed, and I can relate to that prayer. A prayer asking God to end it all (19:4). I cannot change. I have been through so many years of intercession, deliverance, fasting, healing conferences etc, but I am still gay, and I am exhausted trying to be somebody that I am not. If God is not going to change me and He expects me to be straight, then life is unfair, and God is unfair too. God cannot demand things of me, of us, and not help us to do His will. Then I am doomed, I have no future, and He is playing cruel games with our lives.

I prayed that prayer many times. I was not suicidal, and I was not trying to end my life, but I asked God to do it. I could not face hurting my family through a divorce. I could not face continuing hurting my family if we did not divorce. Therefore, the logical conclusion was that if I was not there anymore, then there would be no disasters, no humiliation of my family, no more attacks from the Christian community. I wanted a way out like Elijah. Elijah and I, we had had enough.

This is a very lonely place to be. Elijah was in the wilderness and I was in my personal wilderness. Nowhere to feel safe. Nowhere to really call home. This loneliness was killing me slowly. I was so broken that it was difficult to be open to anybody because I did not know what would come out. I was bursting with pain; I was crippled in my soul and spirit. People noticed that something was going on, but what could I say? I can see why Elijah left his servant and visited the wilderness on his own. At least, he did not have to pretend that he had it all together. He did not even have to try.

In this disquieted state, an angel inspired Elijah to take care of himself (19:5-8). He had to eat and drink because the next stage of his life was going to be a tough one. Not only had he just been through quite a spiritual battle, but it was not over yet. There was more to come, even though he was in a depleted state emotionally and physically.

He ate, drank, and slept. He did the basics, so he was ready for 40 tiresome days. At least his challenges lasted only for 40 days. For some of us, they take much longer.

I have become aware of the importance of taking care of myself in good times, but also in times of trouble when I do not have the energy to do so. If I do not, then my blood pressure rises, my weight goes up, my sleep is disturbed, I produce too many red blood cells, and the list goes on. Then I am in the predicament that not only is my emotional life on fire, my body is out of control, too. I had to face the music and decide what to do: Was I going to sit in my wilderness and sulk, or was I going to protect myself from bad habits? When the bad habits move in, then body-shaming moves in along with them. Guilt, shame, and sadness are not infrequent visitors in such times, and they have a destructive influence on me.

I am learning that I can take positive steps, especially in fearful times. After being ousted from the church, I had some serious decisions to make. I looked at the scales and did not like the result. My blood pressure was not good either. I made decisions about my diet, sleeping patterns, etc. Little things, small steps – and sometimes big steps - but they all led in the right direction. It might take time, but I told myself it was a good investment for the present and for the future.

I developed new spiritual habits. I bought an orthodox knot chain and I pray my personalised version of the Jesus prayer daily. When I go for long walks, I bring my prayer chain, and I pray for an hour or two. I started reading about Ignatian spirituality and practicing the Examen daily. I read spiritual books, have bought a few new Bible translations, I am attending several LGBT+ conferences and retreats, and I am writing this book and have done the research for another. I wanted God to be at the centre of this period of my life. In this time of crisis, I did not want to give up on God and fill the void and the loneliness with entertainment and unhealthy habits. Now, years later, I am getting ready for the next chapter of my life.

Ignatius of Loyola encouraged us to build up our spiritual life during times of consolation, so we have a reservoir of deep encounters with God for times of desolation. I have learnt that we can also develop a deeper spirituality in times of desolation, because God meets us with His grace. We are not left alone in our solitude. I have noticed how this time in my life has been the most spiritually rewarding time, even though many things have not fallen into place yet and I still bother God many times a day with some of the same prayer requests. There are some very deep longings in my heart that I take boldly to God, because I have realised that He cares.

We notice that God is asking Elijah the same question twice (19:9, 13). "Elijah, what are you doing here?" Reading his answer, we can see that Elijah gave the same answer (19:10, 14). He had been fighting for God, but now he was alone! Elijah felt as if he was on a one-man mission impossible for God. There was nobody like him and he was in fear of his life.

It did not matter that God showed himself to him. His answer was the same: I am a one-man band. Loneliness is a silent killer. It permeates our soul and takes over our imagination. Loneliness is more common than we think, but we rarely talk about it. Instead, we may become obsessive of our friends and family. We love them to death. We demand so much from them that they suffocate or maybe we become bitter. Elijah was bitter, he was angry, and he was depressed. Ministry was not all that was set out to be. Life sucked, according to Elijah.

Like Elijah we may get God wrong, but I think it is encouraging to see how God tried to get Elijah's attention on several occasions. First, He sent angels, then He asked Elijah to stand on the mountain and be on the lookout.

I love the way God was redirecting Elijah's attention. This can help us to understand what is happening to us in tough times. God let Elijah face the wind, the earthquake, and the fire, but God was not in any of those. We expect God to show up with a bang, but doesn't that rather tell us about our fears? When we face problems, it is difficulty to stand in the wind, because situations try to do away with us. When we have found our feet again, then the next wave starts. Here the illustration is an earthquake where even the ground is unsafe. We are forced to move on, in the same was as I ended up moving from the UK to Denmark to reboot my life. I do not know at the time of writing (2018), if this is permanent or transitory, but it was as if there was no rock under my feet. Everything that I knew was blown to pieces.

And God goes on as if this was not enough. Expect that even the fire might show up to burn away all evidence of things we have done and who we are. The wind, the earthquake, and the fire are all powerful, but God can use them to refine us. We get a new start, a clean slate. Would I have chosen another route, no doubt about it, but God used the winding road, the path of tears to create something new. I found God, a loving God. I thought I had known Him since I gave my life to Him when I was 17 years old, but now I know Him so much more intimately. I have moved from respecting God, being afraid of

God to loving God. And the best thing is that now I know that he loves me too.

After all the trials, God came in the refreshing breeze (19:12). It is easy to overlook Him, because of all the emotional stuff going on. He brings peace while we are in pain. He brings hope during the disasters. He brings love to soothe my hurting soul. He is truly the Great Counsellor, Almighty God, Everlasting Father, and the Prince of Peace. He touches my life gently, so I do not get bruised and feel spiritually violated by Him. The world, the false spirit has violated my boundaries, but God heals me with His gentle breeze: His words of love, and His gifts of grace (for me the first steps were a home, a job, and a church where I could worship and minister).

For Elijah this was not enough. He had not changed. He felt the pain and the alienation. He gave the same answer to the same question. He had not moved on emotionally or spiritually.

Then God chose to send him on his way (19:15-16). He gave him a job to do. Something that he could recognise. Something he had done before. It was time to anoint people for ministry. God showed Elijah that his time was not over. He might have a target on his back, but it should not stop him from doing ministry for God.

Recently, I met an angel. I had been to my home church in the morning but decided to visit another church as well where they were having a jazz worship service. It was a church that, as far as I know, do not encourage, or believe in exercising the gifts of the Spirit.

The worship service was in English and especially for tourists. I attended the service and enjoyed the music. The jazz music created a wonderful atmosphere. When the service was over, a lady came up to me. I had not noticed her during the service. She would have stood out though, as she was one out of only two black people in church that day, but I did not see her. She told me that she had been praying for me during the service and she had three points for me. She talked about me being a shepherd in the eyes of God, how I would be like Moses using my shepherd's staff to protect and provide for people, how I should know that God would be my shepherd as we read about Him in Psalm 23, but that I was also that kind of shepherd in God's eyes to other people.

As soon as she had finished, she just left the church. I tried to talk to her, but she just turned around and went away. It was like an angel just showing up, encouraging me, and then leaving when she had done her job.

I wanted to tell her how much I was longing to be a pastor again, how I had enquired about a position in the UK, and much more. I did not get the chance to do that. The angel had left the building.

I had never dreamt in a thousand years that I would receive a word of knowledge by attending this jazz worship service. I just stood there, smiling, and thanking God. I was bursting. I felt God was saying to me that I was a pastor in His eyes, and that He wanted to use me as a pastor again. I would see miracles like Moses and much, much more.

Like Elijah, God is sending me back to the mission field. Back to something that I know. He was telling me that my calling had not come to an end when I came out.

As I reflected on this, I was reminded of the book title by Troy Perry who founded the Metropolitan Community church. It is called, "The Lord is My Shepherd and He Knows I'm Gay." Recently, a denomination refused to consider me as a pastor because I am gay, but God said to me through a stranger, an angel, that my ministry is not over, and He knows I am gay.

About the Author

REV. **D**R. **A**RNO **Steen Andreasen** is the co-president of the European Forum of LGBT Christian Groups. He has been a pioneering pastor, overseer of a network of churches, managing director, and social entrepreneur for decades. With a calling to preach, train leaders, and write books, he is passionate about developing thought-provoking training projects and qualifications as well as health and social projects.